From the Roer to the Elbe With the 1st Medical Group: Medical Support of the Deliberate River Crossing

by
Captain Donald E. Hall

U.S. Army Command and General Staff College
Fort Leavenworth, Kansas 66027-6900

COMBAT
STUDIES
INSTITUTE

Library of Congress Cataloging-in-Publication Data

Hall, Donald E. (Donald Edward), 1959-

    From the Roer to the Elbe with the 1st Medical Group : medical support of the deliberate river crossing / by Donald E. Hall.

    p.   cm.

    Includes bibliographical references.

    1. United States. Army. Medical Corps. Medical Group, 1st—History. 2. World War, 1939-1945—Regimental histories—United States. 3. World War, 1939-1945—Medical care—United States. 4. World War, 1939-1945—Medical care—Germany. 5. World War, 1939-1945—Campaigns—Germany. 6. Stream crossing, Military—History—20th century. I. Title.
D807.U6H35 1992
940.54'7573—dc20   91-30329
                                                  CIP

The smallest detail, taken from actual incident in war, is more instructive to me, a soldier, than all the Thiers and Jominis in the world.

— ARDANT DU PICQ
Battle Studies

CONTENTS

CONTENTS

ILLUSTRATIONS

Figures

Maps

PREFACE

The seeds of this paper were first planted in early 1986 by Colonel Henry J. Waters, Medical Service Corps (MSC), and the late Lieutenant Colonel Harold G. Block, MSC, then commander and executive officer of the 1st Medical Group, Fort Hood, Texas. Both suggested that I do some work on the group's history; they said that it might be fun. In line with these suggestions, I hope eventually to expand my work to include a complete history of the 1st Medical Regiment-1st Medical Group from 1917 to 1945.

This current study was prepared while I was holding the fellowship in military medical history at the Uniformed Services University of the Health Sciences, Bethesda, Maryland, from August 1988 to August 1989. I am grateful to Dr. Robert J. T. Joy, M.D. (Col., Medical Corps, USA, ret.), chairman of the Section of Medical History at the university, for support, advice, and editorial review.

This paper relies rather heavily on primary source material, and several persons greatly assisted me in accessing archival sources. Of most help was Mr. Richard Boylan, chief of the Modern Military Records Branch of the National Archives, in the Washington National Records Center, Suitland, Maryland. His detailed knowledge of records relating to the Army Medical Department and its field units during the war uncovered several key documents for me that I might not otherwise have found. On several occasions, Albert E. Cowdrey, Ph.D., chief of the Special Histories Branch of the Center of Military History, U.S. Army, made documents filed in his office available to me. Richard J. Sommers, Ph.D., and his staff in the archives of the U.S. Army Military History Institute, Carlisle Barracks, Pennsylvania (housed, interestingly enough, in the former classroom building of the Medical Field Service School), were most helpful during my review of the William E. Shambora and Paul R. Hawley Papers in their holdings.

Several veterans of the 1st Medical Regiment and the 1st Medical Group were also of assistance. Al Gruenberg and Harold Schroeder provided me with membership rosters of the 1st Medical Regiment Association. Thomas S. Prideaux, Harry L. Gans (Col., MSC, USA, ret.), and Malcolm D. Blankenship all answered questions on their experiences in the 1st Medical

Group during the war. Louis H. Veigel and Judith (Veigel) Hall, brother and daughter of the late Colonel Lester P. Veigel, provided information on him otherwise no longer obtainable.

Dale C. Smith, Ph.D., and the late Dr. Peter D. Olch, M.D., of the Section of Medical History, Uniformed Services University of the Health Sciences; Major David W. Cannon, MSC, formerly of the Academy of Health Sciences, U.S. Army; and Captain Karin E. Neergaard, MSC, of the Walter Reed Army Institute of Research are all now more thoroughly knowledgeable of the history of the 1st Medical Regiment than they ever cared to be. Their interest in this project and their willingness to listen to my occasionally incoherent ramblings helped me to focus my thoughts on this project and eliminated the need for several preliminary drafts of this paper that might otherwise have been necessary.

Most of the sources referenced in this paper are primary sources—documents generated by the 1st Medical Group or some other agency during the war. Copies of a number of the sources are found in more than one location. For example, copies of the *Period Report of Medical Activities, 1st Semi-Annual—1945, 1st Medical Group* are located in the unit historical files of the 1st Medical Group, Fort Hood, Texas; the Special Histories Branch, U.S. Army Center of Military History, Washington, DC; and in Record Groups 112 and 407 of the National Archives. This is typical of many of the documents referenced in this study. In cases such as this, my policy was, first, to cite the most complete existing copy; second, if several copies were equally complete, to cite the original or most legible copy (since these documents were generated in the days before the advent of photocopy machines, some carbon copies were nearly illegible); and finally, if several copies were equally complete and legible, to cite the most readily accessible copy. Monthly after-action reports that I have cited were normally found as enclosures to annual historical reports; in these cases, the base document is not cited, only the after-action report. In all cases, enough information is provided to assist the interested reader in locating the report.

I. INTRODUCTION

The deliberate river-crossing operation is one of the most difficult tasks facing a ground combat commander. Forcing his way across a formidable natural barrier, expanding a bridgehead, and moving additional combat forces and their logistical support into the bridgehead for subsequent breakout—all compete for a commander's attention.[1] The medical planner also faces special problems in securing the movement of casualties from the bridgehead to treatment facilities. Yet little if any attention is devoted to these operations in Army Medical Department doctrinal literature or training courses. This leaves the modern health-services support planner only one place to turn for guidance—the past. In this paper, I shall examine the experiences of the U.S. 1st Medical Group and the support it provided to the XIII Corps in its crossing of the Roer River in late February 1945 and the XVI Corps in its crossing of the Rhine River in March 1945.

Background

The 1st Medical Group was originally organized in France in 1917 as the 1st Sanitary Train and provided division-level health-services support to the 1st Division. After participating in six campaigns with the division during the war[2] and in the occupation of Germany following the armistice, the unit returned to the United States on 25 August 1919. On 10 February 1921, the unit was reorganized and redesignated the 1st Medical Regiment. When the units of the 1st Division were scattered to posts along the eastern seaboard, the regiment was ordered to Carlisle Barracks, Pennsylvania, where it served as the demonstration unit for the newly established Medical Field Service School.[3] The regiment would remain there until 15 June 1940, when it moved to Camp Ord, California.[4] To serve with the regiment while it was at Carlisle Barracks was considered one of the most desirable assignments in the Medical Department, and many of the senior Medical Department officers during World War II had served in the 1st Medical Regiment, including virtually the entire medical chain of supervision of the 1st Medical Group in Europe.

The regiment had always trained hard. It had participated in the First Army maneuvers at Pine Camp, New York, in 1935; in the First Army maneuvers in August 1939; and in the Third Army maneuvers in Texas and Louisiana in April through June

1

The Medical Field Service School, Carlisle Barracks, 1940

1940. In the Texas-Louisiana maneuvers, the regiment completed the 2,900-mile round-trip from Carlisle Barracks to Texas and back a mere eleven days before departing on its permanent change of station move to Camp Ord, California.[5]

While the 1st Medical Regiment was continuing its training, the headquarters of the Army Ground Forces—responsible for organizing, equipping, and training units for their deployment overseas—was planning substantial changes in the organization of corps and field armies. The organization of these units would no longer be a fixed one, with a set number of divisions per corps, corps per field army, and a fixed support organization organic to the field army. Rather, organizations would become flexible, with units attached or detached as required to support tactical operations. All fixed nondivisional units—until then primarily regiments and separate battalions—were replaced with a building-block concept: separate battalions of the combat arms and separate companies of the combat support and combat service support branches would be task organized under separate group and battalion headquarters. Planners believed this would allow for the most efficient use of assets and provide greater flexibility to the ground combat commander.[6]

In accordance with this reorganization, the 1st Medical Regiment was broken up on 1 September 1943. The Headquarters and Service Company was reorganized and redesignated as the Headquarters and Headquarters Detachment, 1st Medical Group, and its subordinate companies were reorganized and redesignated as separate medical companies.[7] Although the reorganiza-

Colonel William E. Shambora, U.S.
Ninth Army Surgeon

tion was not accepted wholeheartedly by the entire Army
Medical Department, the 1st Medical Group, while in Europe,
would serve under the Ninth Army Surgeon, Colonel William
E. Shambora. Colonel Shambora had been the Army Ground
Forces Surgeon at the time of the reorganization and supported
the reorganization. He had, in fact, requested reassignment from
the Army Ground Forces to a field army headquarters so that
he could see for himself how well the system worked—and he
was quite pleased with the results.[8]

Shambora had entered the Army Medical Department in
1925, shortly after receiving his M.D. degree from Georgetown
University. After completing an internship at Fitzsimmons
General Hospital, he held a variety of assignments, including
tours as a company commander in the 1st and 12th Medical
Regiments and as executive officer, S3, and adjutant of the 2d
Medical Regiment at Fort Sam Houston, Texas. From 1937 to
1941, when he was reassigned to the Office of the Army Ground
Forces Surgeon, he served as an instructor at the Medical Field
Service School, first in the Department of Military Arts and
later as both director of the Department of Logistics and as
commander of the 32d Medical Battalion, the unit that had
replaced the 1st Medical Regiment as the demonstration unit
for the school. He completed the two-year course at the U.S.
Army Command and General Staff School in 1935 and the
Army War College in 1938.[9] He was probably well known to

Maj. Gen. Paul R. Hawley, Surgeon of the European Theater of Operations

the Surgeon of the European Theater of Operations, Major General Paul R. Hawley. Hawley's tour as a student at the Command and General Staff School had overlapped the second year of Shambora's, and Hawley had served as commander of the 1st Medical Regiment, director of the Department of Administration, and assistant commandant of the Medical Field Service School during Shambora's tenure as an instructor and department director at Carlisle.[10]

The group continued to train, supporting a number of large-scale exercises that required the headquarters to make a permanent change of station to Camp Carson, Colorado, and later to Fort Riley, Kansas. When the headquarters finally received orders to move overseas, the news was well received, according to one informal history of the group:

> The morale was better than it had ever been, lifted above "excellent" by the realization that at last the unit was moving toward the service for which it had been training at Fort Ord, Camp White, Oregon, Camp Carson, Colorado, and Camp Funston [on the Fort Riley reservation], Kansas. "I'd begun to think the old 1st Medical Regiment's marching song, you know, the part that said 'we train, we train, and then we train some more,' was going to be our motto for life," one sergeant said, "Now, it's just to [sic] blamed good to be true that we're on our way."[11]

The group moved to the Boston Port of Embarkation and on 7 October 1944 sailed for France aboard the transport *Mount Vernon*.[12] About two weeks prior to their departure, the group staff had been informed that they would be assigned to the U.S. Ninth Army, already in Europe.[13] While the word of their assignment was spread among the officers, the men had no idea of their destination:

> Rumors were in spite of all directives to the contrary, sending the unit to all parts of the globe. It was going "direct to India via the Mediterranean", "to Britain to re-stage", "to Britain for immediate shipment to France", "direct to France", "direct to Southern France for incorporation with a new army now forming". It was rumored that "trade goods" should fill all optional space in luggage since money meant nothing over there. Special emphasis was placed on liquor (worth a hundred dollars a bottle), "Soap" is a universal bartering item, and lipstick runs a close second to silk stockings, as an international currency.[14]

Since the 1st Medical Group had spent several years on the West Coast, and all of the other units that had been part of the 1st Medical Regiment had been deployed to the southwest Pacific, the rumors concerning its varied destinations were probably inevitable.

Arriving in England on 15 October 1944,[15] the headquarters was loaded onto the South African liner *Llangibby Castle* and

Courtesy of Harry L. Gans (Col., USA, ret.)

The men of the 1st Medical Group set up pup tents on their initial entrance into France

Surgeon Jonathan Letterman, medical director of the Army of the Potomac during the Civil War

sailed for France on 17 October,[16] landing on Omaha Beach on 18 October, where "Lt Col Veigel [the group commander], near the bow [of the landing craft transporting them to shore from the *Llangibby Castle*] for the privilege, was the first of the detachment to go ashore. He'd brought with him the descendants of the 1st Sanitary Train, that had evacuated the 1st Division in World War One."[17] After a long period in the arrival staging area, uneventful save for the loss of the officers' footlockers, the 1st Medical Group moved into the Ninth Army zone. There, it was committed in support of the XIII Corps on 25 November 1944.[18] The oldest color-bearing unit in the Army Medical Department was again, at last, at war.

Health Services Support Doctrine—1945

While the medical support system used by the United States Army in 1945 was, as it is today, basically a modification of the system originally developed by Surgeon Jonathan Letterman, medical director of the Army of the Potomac in 1863,[19] there were a number of significant differences from the system used today. To place the 1st Medical Group's operations in the proper context, a review of the system in use in 1945 is presented here.

The health-services support system in 1945 was, as it is today, divided into five levels of care, called echelons. The first echelon of care, then as today, was unit-level health-services support. It began at the site of injury or illness and included self/buddy aid, treatment by the company aidman, and treatment at the battalion or regimental aid station (see appendix for the chain of casualty evacuation).[20] In the infantry regiment, this echelon of care was provided by a regimental medical detachment of 10 officers and 126 enlisted men. The section was divided into a headquarters section, which operated the regimental aid station, and three battalion sections, each of which provided a battalion aid station, litter bearers, and company aidmen to one of the battalions organic to the regiment.[21] The regimental aid station was organized in much the same manner as the battalion aid stations, with the addition of two Dental Corps officers. Because its capabilities and level of care were the same as that found in the battalion aid station, patients would not normally be evacuated from the battalion aid station to the regimental aid station. Rather, patients would be evacuated from the battalion aid station to the division collecting company, while the regimental aid station would provide care for personnel in the regimental rear area.[22] In the other branches of the combat arms, these functions were performed by battalion medical detachments. Many of the units in the combat support branches also had organic medical detachments.[23] As World War II went on, it was found that the dental officers in the infantry regiments were underutilized and in many cases, they were removed from the regiments and used to form roving dental teams that provided dental care for a geographic area, rather than for specific units.[24]

The second echelon of support, division-level health-services support, was provided in the infantry and armored division by the division's organic medical battalion. The battalion had two types of companies—collecting companies and clearing companies. Organic to the battalion were three collecting companies and a clearing company. The collecting companies had ambulance and litter-bearer sections and were responsible for evacuating casualties from the regiments to the division clearing station.[25] Normally, patients were evacuated by ambulance from the battalion aid stations, but if the terrain or the tactical situation would not permit this, they would be transported by the litter-bearer section from the battalion aid station to a collecting station established by the collecting company. There, they would be inspected by a Medical Corps officer, given emergency treatment if required, and then placed on ambulances for transport to the division clearing station.[26] At the clearing station established by the clearing company, patients were triaged (or sorted), and those who required care beyond the capabilities of the clearing station were prepared for transport to third-echelon treatment facilities, with emergency resuscitative care provided as required. Patients who would be returned to duty in a short period of time—usually a few hours—would be held at the station until released.[27] This system is similar to the forward-support/main-support medical company concept we currently employ.

Second-echelon care for nondivisional troops assigned or attached to a corps was provided by a separate medical battalion assigned to the corps, which also provided first-echelon care to those units that lacked an organic medical detachment. In the army area, first- and second-echelon care was provided to units without an organic capability to provide such care by one of the medical groups assigned to the army.

The third echelon of medical support in World War II was the equivalent of what we today would call corps-level medical support but was provided during the war by the field army. This was because the corps, as employed in World War II, served only as a tactical headquarters, with little or no logistic or administrative capability. There was no overall medical command and control headquarters at this echelon. All third-echelon medical units were under the direct command of the army commander and under the technical supervision of the army surgeon.[28] In the Ninth Army, of which the 1st Medical Group was a component, Colonel Shambora was delegated to command all army medical units not placed under the control of a subordinate command of the army.[29] The third echelon of health-services support had three major missions. The first of these missions was to provide first- and second-echelon health-services support to those units in the army area that lacked organic medical assets. The second mission was evacuation of patients from second-echelon treatment facilities, and the third mission was hospitalization.

To provide for the first mission, the field army had assigned to it separate, numbered clearing and collecting companies. (See the glossary for the functions of various medical components of the Ninth Army.) The separate medical clearing company provided clearing support for up to 15,000 troops or support or reinforcement to divisional clearing elements. The basis of allocation for this unit was one company per supported division.[30] The mission of the separate medical collecting company was essentially the same as its divisional counterpart: to collect patients by litter or ambulance from first-echelon treatment facilities, provide them with needed stabilizing treatment at the collecting station, and then transport them by ambulance to a supporting clearing company. In addition to collecting patients in the corps or army area, the company could also be used to support a divisional medical battalion with additional collecting assets. The normal basis of allocation was one company per supported division.[31]

To accomplish the second third-echelon mission—evacuation from second-echelon treatment facilities—the army used separate, numbered motor-ambulance companies. The motor-ambulance company's mission was to evacuate patients from second-echelon medical facilities belonging to divisional medical battalions or nondivisional clearing or collecting companies to third-echelon hospitals belonging to the field army. The basis of allocation of this unit was one company per 12,000 supported troops.[32] These separate collecting, clearing, and motor-ambulance companies would be organized under separate medical battalions, which were in turn organized under a medical group headquarters, generally on the basis of one medical group per corps supported by the army.

The medical group and separate battalion headquarters were similar in organization and function. The group headquarters was composed of ten officers and twenty-four enlisted men. The commander (a colonel) and the executive officer (a lieutenant colonel) were both Medical Corps officers; the rest of the officers in the headquarters were Medical Administrative Corps officers. The headquarters provided command and control for six to eight subordinate battalions, companies, or separate units.[33]

The separate medical battalion headquarters was composed of six officers, one warrant officer, and twenty-two enlisted men. With the exception of the commander and executive officer (who were Medical Corps officers) and the personnel-services warrant officer, all officers of the headquarters were Medical Administrative Corps officers. The battalion provided command and control for three to six subordinate medical companies and provided maintenance and personnel-services support to its subordinate units through sections formed by attaching mechanics and clerks to the battalion from companies under its control.[34]

The final service provided by third-echelon health-services support was hospitalization. To provide this service, the field army used three types of hospitals: the 750-bed evacuation hospital, the 400-bed evacuation hospital (semimobile), and the field hospital. The evacuation hospital had almost no mobility through its organic transportation assets, nor was its staff

An evacuation hospital in France (World War II)

trained in unit movements. It was essentially a fixed medical installation designed to be moved infrequently.[35]

The evacuation hospital (semimobile) was a 400-bed facility with the same mission as the 750-bed evacuation hospital.[36] One important difference between the two was that the semimobile evacuation hospital was equipped with more trucks than the evacuation hospital, making it about 25 percent mobile in organic transportation assets. Additionally, the staff was trained in moving the facility and could move in eight to ten hours (after all patients had been removed) and could reestablish the facility in four to six hours after arriving at a new location.[37]

The field hospital was especially valuable, as it could be established as a single 400-bed facility or as three 100-bed facilities, which gave the army surgeon a great deal of flexibility in providing needed health-services support.[38] The field hospital was considered a semimobile station hospital designed to provide "definitive surgical and medical treatment to troops in the theater of operations where fixed facilities [did] not exist, and where construction of fixed facilities [was] undesirable."[39]

In practice, the hospital units of the field hospital were often employed in close proximity to a division clearing station, where they could provide more definitive care than that available in the division—much the same way in which mobile army surgical hospitals would be employed in Korea a few years later. The lack of sufficient surgeons and nurses in the hospital units of the field hospital was, in fact, one of several factors leading to the development of the mobile army surgical hospital after the war.[40]

A hodgepodge of additional units, serving directly under the army surgeon, provided medical logistics, laboratory, veterinary, and other ancillary services to the army.[41] The most important of these units was probably the medical depot company. Commanded by a lieutenant colonel, the company—with 13 officers, 1 warrant officer, and 136 enlisted men organized into a headquarters, a maintenance platoon, and 3 storage platoons—was the equivalent of the modern medical-supply, optical, and maintenance (MEDSOM) battalion. The three storage and issue platoons gave the company the ability to provide continuous support while displacing over large lateral distances. The company's mission was to provide third- and fourth-level medical maintenance of medical equipment; to replace and repair spectacles and dental prosthetic appliances; and to receive, store, and issue medical supplies in support of 125,000 combat-zone troops.[42]

Also found in the field army, and helping to partially counteract the lack of physicians in the field hospital, was an assortment of surgical augmentation teams. There were seven types of surgical teams in World War II, all organized under the blanket Table of Organization and Equipment 8-55, *Professional Services*. These included team EA, general surgery; team EB, orthopedic surgery; team ED, maxillofacial surgery; team

A field hospital in the Mediterranean theater (World War II)

In World War II, general hospitals were sometimes set up in tents (example from Constantine, Algeria)

EE, neurosurgery; and team EF, thoracic surgery—each of the above with three officers, one nurse, and three enlisted men. There were also team EC, shock treatment, with one officer, one nurse, and three enlisted men, and team EG, gas treatment, with one officer and three enlisted men. The EA through EF teams provided, in effect, additional staffed operating tables for the facilities to which they were attached, while team EG provided oxygen therapy for lung-irritant casualties. The teams were organized under a headquarters to form an auxiliary surgical group; the Fifth Auxiliary Surgical Group supported the Ninth Army.

The fourth echelon of care corresponded to what we today would call communications zone—or echelons above corps— medical support. It was provided in 1,000-bed or larger general hospitals, usually grouped together in hospital centers, station hospitals, and convalescent centers. With an evacuation policy sometimes as long as 120 days, this echelon of care was designed to return the maximum number of patients to duty within the theater.[43]

The fifth echelon of care formed the hospital base in the United States. A patient returned from an overseas theater would receive care in one of sixty-six named general hospitals,[44] numerous station hospitals, convalescent centers, or in Veterans Administration facilities. As a general rule, a patient would not be evacuated to the United States unless his injuries required an extremely long convalescent period, the equipment or facilities were not available to treat his injuries in theater, or his injuries would result in his being medically discharged upon recovery.[45]

Governing all medical planning were a series of general doctrinal rules, most of which are as valid today as they were in 1945:

1. Commanders of all echelons are responsible for the provision of adequate and proper medical care for all noneffectives [persons whose medical condition prevents them from performing their military duties] of their command.

2. Medical service is continuous.

3. Sick or injured individuals go no farther to the rear than their condition or the medical situation warrants.

4. Sorting of the fit from the unfit takes place at each medical installation in the chain of evacuation.

5. Casualties in the combat zone are collected at medical installations along the general axis of advance of the units to which they pertain.

6. Medical units must possess and retain tactical mobility to permit them to move to positions on the battlefield and enable them to move in support of combat elements.

An example of a general hospital in a fully established site (at Pistoia, Italy)

7. Mobility of medical installations in the combat zone is dependent upon prompt and continuous evacuation by higher medical echelons.

8. The size of medical installations increases and the necessity and ability to move decreases the farther from the front lines these units are located.

9. Medical units must be disposed so as to render the greatest service to the greatest number.[46]

These doctrinal statements should be kept in mind by the reader during the discussion of medical support that follows.

Command and Control

One problem with the medical organization used in World War II was the lack of an overall medical command and control headquarters at the third and fourth echelons of health-services support—a problem not completely and adequately addressed by the Medical Department until well into the 1960s.[47] In support of a typical corps was a separate medical battalion—under the command of the corps commander and the technical supervision of the corps surgeon—which provided second-echelon care to non-divisional units assigned or attached to the corps. Patients were evacuated from the corps' divisions and from its attached medical battalion by a medical group of the field army—in this case, under the command of the army commander and the technical supervision of the army surgeon. The medical group also provided second-echelon health-services support to the units of the army operating in the corps area but not attached to the corps. The group evacuated patients to the evacuation hospitals of the field army, again under the command of the army commander and the technical supervision of his surgeon. This meant that health-services support for the corps was provided, for the most part, by units not under the control of the corps. In turn, the medical groups evacuated casualties to hospitals not under their control—hospitals that sometimes received patients from more than one corps. A lack of close coordination at any point could have created disastrous results for the wounded.

To prevent such problems in the Ninth Army, Colonel Shambora held weekly meetings at the army headquarters with his corps surgeons, hospital commanders, and medical group commanders, where he discussed problem areas and support of future operations (with occasional additional meetings as required by the circumstances).[48] The XIII Corps Surgeon, Colonel Dean Schamber, held similar weekly meetings at his office with his division surgeons, his medical battalion commander, and the "supporting medical group commander"[49]—as did the XVI Corps Surgeon, Colonel Thomas Furlong.[50] A review of unit and staff section journals for these headquarters shows a constant flow of visitors (commanders, staff officers, and liaison officers) among the headquarters involved. While problems would still occur, most notably during the Roer River crossings, this coordination no doubt prevented many problems before they could affect patient care.

II. OPERATION GRENADE, THE ROER RIVER CROSSING

As it had since 28 November 1944, the Ninth Army, on 1 February 1945, stood poised on the banks of the Roer River. Most of the Ninth's divisions had been transferred to the First Army to allow it to counterattack the German offensive effort in the Ardennes.[51] This offensive, along with greater than anticipated resistance by the Germans during the Ninth Army's advance to the Roer, had prevented the assault on the Roer from being a continuation of the army's November offensive. One major obstacle still remained—the Roer River dams. These dams, and in particular the concrete Urft dam near Gemeund and the earthen Schwammenauel dam near Hasenfeld—both in the First Army's area of operations—were of particular concern to planners, for if these dams were destroyed while a friendly force remained on the east bank of the Roer, the resulting floods would wash out any tactical bridges supporting the force, allowing it to be defeated in detail.[52] The Ninth Army engineer estimated that, in the worst case, destruction of the dams would make the Roer impassable in the Ninth Army's zone for in excess of fourteen days.[53] This fact was well known to both the Allies and the Germans, and the Allies had repeatedly attempted either to destroy the dams by bombardment or to capture them intact— all to no avail. Finally, early on 10 February 1945, the First Army captured the dams, only to find that the retreating Germans had destroyed the discharge valves allowing water to flow through the dams uncontrolled.[54] Fortunately for the Ninth Army, Lieutenant General William H. Simpson, Ninth Army commander, had on 9 February postponed the attack scheduled for 0530 on the 10th. Had the attack taken place as scheduled, the assault forces would have been trapped on the far side of the river.[55] The flood caused by the damaged dams resulted in the river rising an average of 5 feet and increasing in width, depending on the terrain, to between 400 and 1,200 yards. The river's velocity increased to an average speed of ten and a half feet per second—all of which made rafting operations virtually impossible.[56] The resultant delay, while disappointing, allowed the army staff to refine their plans and to increase their stockpiles of supplies and ammunition.

On 1 February 1945, the medical situation in the Ninth Army was well in hand. Because of a disagreement over a hospital location the previous December, the Ninth Army Surgeon, Colonel

The Schwammenauel dam on the Roer River posed a threat to U.S. troops and the tactical bridges they built to ford the river

Shambora, had obtained an agreement from General Simpson that medical units would have priority in choosing their sites whenever army units displaced.[57] Evacuation of casualties was proceeding without problems, and the army and corps surgeons' staffs were busily preparing for the support of the Roer crossing. The Roer River crossing, in addition to being a major problem, had added significance for future operations. The army staff, from General Simpson on down, saw the real obstacle as the Rhine River crossing and the subsequent advance to the Elbe. Because of this, they viewed the Roer crossing and the advance to the Rhine as their last opportunity to streamline their operations plan for the Rhine River crossing—almost as though the Roer River crossing were a giant dress rehearsal.[58]

The 1st Medical Group continued to operate smoothly, as it had for the most part since the unit was committed on 25 November 1944.[59] The group's staff had been working together as a team for over a year and a half, as had most of the enlisted men assigned to the headquarters, and this no doubt contributed to the smoothness with which they operated.

The group's commander, Colonel Lester P. Veigel, was a native of Dickinson, North Dakota, who had joined the Medical

Corps in 1932 after receiving his M.D. from Northwestern University in 1931.[60] His assignments included a two-year tour at Carlisle Barracks, after which he attended the Medical Corps' Officer Basic Course in 1934. Following completion of the course, he spent three years at Fort Snelling, Minnesota, and Fort Meade, South Dakota, before being assigned to the Philippines in 1937. Upon his return to the United States in 1940, he was assigned to Fort Lewis, Washington.[61] On 7 August 1943, he assumed command of the 1st Medical Regiment[62] and remained in command of the group when the regiment was broken up the next month. He was promoted to colonel on 19 January 1945, after the 1st Medical Group arrived in Europe.

The group S1 and S2, Major William A. Kran, was a Regular Army master sergeant who had his reserve commission (awarded in 1931) activated on 4 June 1941. He became adjutant of the 1st Medical Regiment in September 1941 and continued in that capacity with the 1st Medical Group. The S4, Major Reuben B. ("Ben") Golub, was a civilian pharmacist in San Diego when he was commissioned in the Medical Administrative Corps and joined the 1st Medical Regiment in 1941 as regimental supply officer; members of the regiment quickly learned that his ire could quickly be raised by asking him: "Why do pharmacists

Lt. Gen. William H. Simpson, commander of U.S. Ninth Army

The commander and staff of the 1st Medical Group: left to right, front row—Maj. William A. Kran (S1 and S2), Col. Lester P. Veigel (commander), and Lt. Col. John D. Dupre (XO); second row—Maj. Reuben B. Golub (S4), Maj. Thomas S. Prideaux (S3), and Chaplain Boldt; third row—Capt. Harry L. Gans (asst. S4, detachment commander), Cpt. Robert Montgomery (asst. S3), 1st Lt. Lester L. Soberg (A&R), and Capt. Kenneth M. Manning (asst. S3 orientation)

charge a dollar for a five-cent prescription?" He and Major Kran must certainly have kept the headquarters lively, for

> How it all began, nobody knows; but for three years Kran and Golub have maintained their private but goodnatured feud, complete with raillery, shouts, and openhanded fisticuffs. The feud notwithstanding, the two were inseparable; and, as a matter of fact, were styled the "Gold-Leaf Twins" when they received their majorities on the same day.[63]

The S3, Major Thomas S. Prideaux, had been a banker in Portland, Oregon, before joining the Army in March 1941. Three months later, he was a sergeant and attending the officer candidate school at Carlisle Barracks. After his commissioning, he was sent to Camp Robinson, Arkansas, as an instructor and joined the group headquarters at the Bend, Oregon, maneuver area on 9 October 1943. He, too, must have helped to keep the headquarters lively, as he was "known as a wit, quick on the 'retort terrible,' but withal able to laugh at his own expense when the occasion arises. Although one of his colleagues once said of him 'Prideaux has no milk of human kindness,' that isn't quite true; the milk is only slightly curdled."[64]

While he left the United States a captain, Prideaux arrived in Europe a major, for on 6 October 1944, while on board the *Mount Vernon*, an impromptu ceremony was held for him:

> A transportation officer came to the Prideaux-Manning stateroom late this evening asking for Captain Prideaux. He brought with him the news, considered urgent enough to wake the sleeping captain, that he was now Major with date of rank of 28 Sept 1944. The message had been relayed by Lt Col Veigel through the Transportation Corps channels. The promotion caught Major Prideaux without the necessary gold leaves to indicate the new rank so another bit of promotion persuaded two majors in an adjacent stateroom to part with the necessary number for one set.[65]

The group executive officer, Lieutenant Colonel John D. Dupre, a reserve Medical Corps officer, was a latecomer to the headquarters. He had replaced the previous executive officer, Lieutenant Colonel Benjamin K. Woro, when the latter was reassigned as commander of the 187th Medical Battalion (then the separate medical battalion for XVIII Airborne Corps) on 7 January 1945. Prior to assuming his duties as group executive

The *Mount Vernon*, the 1st Medical Group's ship on its voyage to France

officer, Lieutenant Colonel Dupre had served as medical inspector of the 84th Infantry Division from 24 September 1942 to 20 July 1943 and as division surgeon of that organization from 21 July 1943 to 13 December 1944.[66]

The staff had made some changes in the internal organization of the headquarters from that authorized in their table of organization and equipment. The table called for one officer to serve as both S1 and S4 and a second to serve as S2 and liaison officer. In field exercises shortly after the 1943 reorganization, the staff found that the work loads of the S1 and S4 resulted in the swamping of that officer, while the S2 duties kept his associate only lightly employed. Accordingly, Colonel Veigel directed that the S1 and S2 duties be combined and the S4 would deal strictly with logistics.[67] January had been a relatively slow month for the 1st Medical Group, with only 1,835 patients transported between facilities,[68] as compared to the 3,948 patients transported during the month of December[69] and the 1,598 patients transported during the 5 days in which the group was operational in November.[70] This gave the staff ample time to plan adequately for the crossings of the Roer and Rhine Rivers.

The organization of the 1st Medical Group on 1 February 1945 was the smallest since it had been committed, as several of its companies had been transferred to other armies to support the Ardennes counteroffensive and had not yet been replaced for the support of the Roer River crossing. The 183d Medical Battalion was composed of the 442d Medical Collecting Company, the 472d Motor Ambulance Company, and the 626th Medical Clearing Company. The group's other medical battalion, the 430th, was composed of 462d Medical Collecting Company and the 488th Motor Ambulance Company (see figure 1).[71]

The 1st Medical Group headquarters was located in the Sisters of St. Joseph Sanitorium in Heerlen, Holland, where it had moved on 12 December 1944 from Valkenburg, Holland, "in order to be better situated, tactically."[72] Living conditions were pleasant. In the words of one unknown member of the headquarters:

> Living conditions were far better than could be expected. We lived in one wing of a sanitorium operated by Catholic Sisters. The men were very satisfied with their quarters and all available means of entertainment were utilized. Radio in sleeping quarters; radio in offices; the Detachment held a dance and party on every second Friday in each month and each party raised morale higher and higher. The men enjoyed these parties as means of relaxation [sic] and

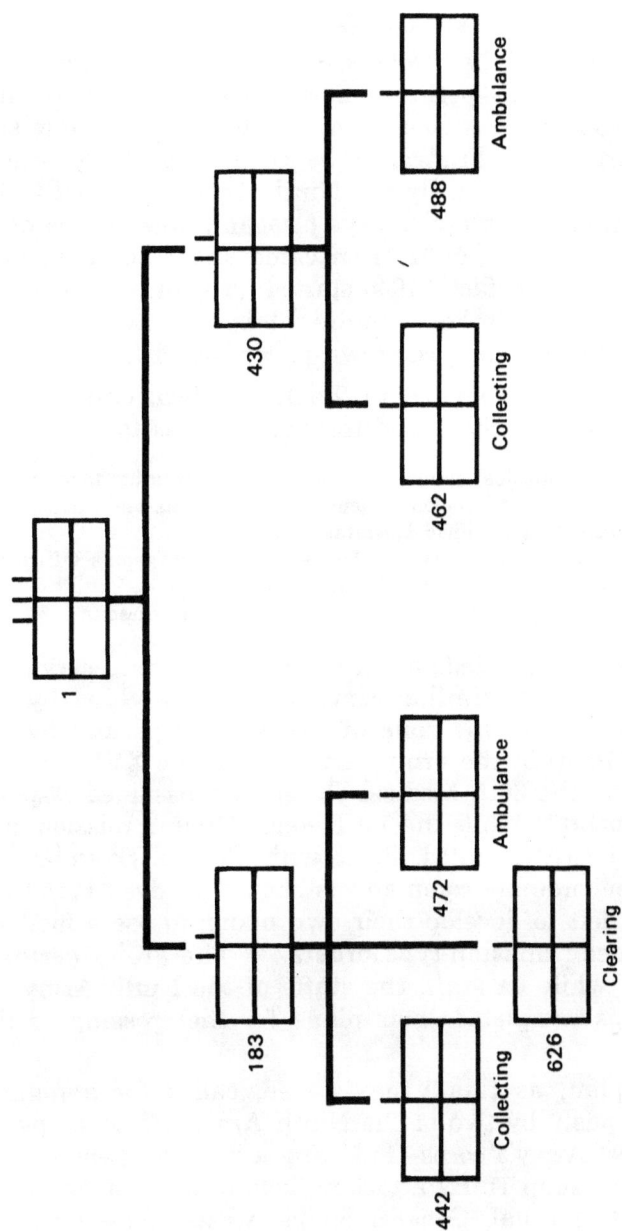

Figure 1. Task organization, 1st Medical Group, 1 February 1945

some of the fellows became well acquainted with some of the local girls of HEERLEN. They visited Dutch homes and gradually learned the customs, and even some, the language of Holland.[73]

The sisters and the sanitorium also provided laundry service to the members of the headquarters,[74] as well as straw mattresses for the men[75] and—perhaps most important of all to the headquarters—access to indoor plumbing for the first time since the group's arrival in France.[76] The code name Cozy assigned to the 1st Medical Group by the Ninth Army appeared to be quite appropriate. All was not always pleasant, however, as on several occasions, the town of Heerlen came under bombing attack by the Luftwaffe.[77] In fact, "1945 started off with a bang, punctuated precisely at the stroke of midnight by the Luftwaffe bombing of the CP [command post] town of HEERLEN, HOLLAND."[78]

The mission assigned to the 1st Medical Group by Colonel Shambora was fairly straightforward. It was to

a. Provide medical service for army units or separate task forces.
b. Provide Third Echelon Evacuation for all units and Fourth Echelon Evacuation for Field Hospital Units.
c. Maintain courier service between Army Surgeon's Office and Division, Corps, and Army Medical Installations.
d. Reinforce Evacuation Hospitals with medical personnel.[79]

While the 1st Medical Group provided these services in the XIII Corps zone, similar services were provided by the 31st Medical Group in the zone of the XIX Corps and by the 30th Medical Group in the army rear.[80] When the XVI Corps became operational, the 30th Medical Group also assumed responsibility for its support.[81] While the 1st Medical Group's mission statement was not overly detailed, it fit with Colonel Shambora's belief that his subordinate commanders should be given broad guidance and then left to develop their own plans; to use a modern term, he provided "mission-type orders."[82] The group performed its missions, while its staff, the staffs of the Ninth Army, and the XIII Corps completed their plans for the crossing of the Roer River.

The plan, as finally envisioned, called for a night attack simultaneously by two of the Ninth Army's three corps and one of the First Army's corps—following a massive 45-minute artillery barrage (see map 1). By attacking before the river had completely returned to normal, General Simpson expected—and achieved—a degree of tactical surprise. After crossing the river, the XIII and XIX Corps would wheel to the north and attack along a corridor between the city of München-Gladbach and the Erft River, allow-

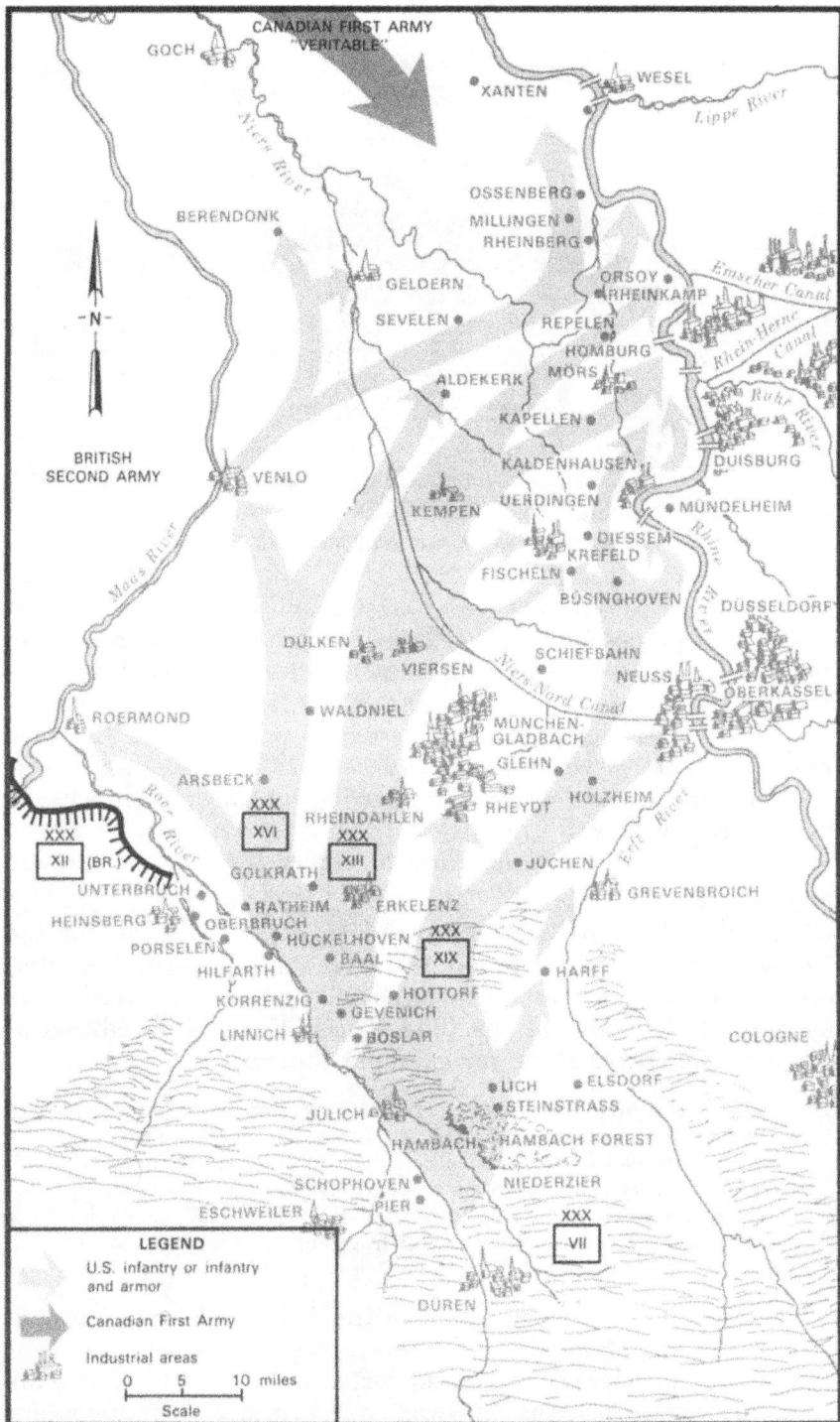

Map 1. Operation Grenade, 23 February—11 March 1945

U.S. troops approaching German positions along the Roer plain

ing the army to outflank the enemy, move swiftly into his rear areas, and pursue him to the Rhine—hopefully capturing one or more bridges across the river intact. After the initial assaults by the XIII and XIX Corps, the XVI Corps would make an unopposed river crossing and serve as the pursuit force. Although enemy resistance was expected to be light to moderate, a contingency plan was developed to provide for unexpectedly heavy resistance. The VII Corps, First Army, would attack simultaneously with the Ninth Army to secure the army's southern flank.[83]

During the war, neither the Ninth Army Surgeon nor the 1st Medical Group's commander issued many formal written orders. While this may seem unusual, it was considered quite appropriate behavior at the time. The 5 March 1941 edition of FM 8-55, *Reference Data*, for example, stated:

> Orders frequently are issued in fragmentary form as the situation develops and supplemental decisions are made. Such fragmentary orders may be extracts from a complete order, or they may cover various phases of an operation successively. A medical battalion or regiment rarely will be able to issue a complete formal order prior to initiating operations. A series of fragmentary orders will be the rule.[84]

Instead, each medical group in the army and each battalion within the 1st Medical Group was given a mission statement and a zone of operations. As supported units entered or left the zone, the proper headquarters was so informed by a fragmentary order. This allowed the units involved to react quickly to rapidly changing situations with a minimum of turbulence. The group also attempted to reduce turbulence by moving its headquarters in echelons. Before closing at one location, the group would become operational via a forward echelon at its new location before informing supported and subordinate units of the move. With the exception of one or two instances when phone service at the new location was inadvertently delayed, the system seemed to work well.[85]

Hospitalization was more complex. Since Colonel Shambora did not like the 750-bed evacuation hospital due to its lack of mobility, the types of hospitals in the Ninth Army zone were limited to field hospitals and 400-bed evacuation hospitals (semi-mobile). The Army Ground Forces Surgeon, Colonel Shambora, once wrote an associate:

> Relative to Evacuation Hospitals, we have but two more 750-bed Evacuation Hospitals left and have not recommended that any more be authorized on the troop basis. I have always visualized them as being too large and cumbersome to be of the greatest value. I am enclosing a T/O [table of organization] and T/E [table of equipment; in World War II they were published as two separate documents] for the 400-bed Evacuation Hospital which you can look over. There is only sufficient transportation allotted to carry organic loads. The unit should be moved by shuttle, part equipment and part personnel, depending upon the situation.[86]

Colonel Shambora often went to great lengths to avoid having 750-bed evacuation hospitals assigned to the Ninth Army. On one of the few occasions when he could not avoid having one attached from the European Theater Services of Supply, he managed to delay the attachment until just before he knew the army would be displacing its rear area forward. Then, as the army displaced, he called the surgeon of the Services of Supply and had the attachment canceled, as the hospital was now in the Services of Supply's support area, not his, and he had no way to move the facility forward to support the army.[87]

The 95th Medical Gas Treatment Battalion, lacking a mission unless the Germans used chemical agents, had its companies employed to provide a combat exhaustion center and a VD treatment center for the army. Combat exhaustion casualties averaged 10 percent of the admissions to division clearing stations, and before the use of the 95th as a combat exhaustion center, 60 percent of them were being evacuated from the army area. Use of the battalion as an exhaustion center and more careful screening in the division area reduced the number of such casualties to 30 percent, or 3 percent of the total admissions to the division clearing stations. In the rapid advances from the Roer to the Rhine, returns to duty within the division of sufferers from combat exhaustion decreased because the clearing stations were displacing so frequently that they were unable to hold patients until they could be returned to duty. However, as those patients who would have been returned to duty within the division were evacuated to the 95th Medical Gas Treatment Battalion, the battalion showed a proportionate increase in the return to duty rates of its patients, causing the total number of combat exhaustion cases being evacuated from the army to remain the same during the Roer and Rhine River crossings.[88] The 8th Convalescent Center completed the hospitalization assets available in the Ninth Army.

The two types of hospitals used in the Ninth Army were employed in vastly different ways. First, the field hospitals, which were being used to provide close support for the divisions (as discussed earlier), were usually placed under the operational control of the medical group in whose operational area they were employed. This was a deviation from doctrine, which saw the medical groups providing the functions originally planned for the medical regiment—collection, clearance, and evacuation—but the system worked well, nonetheless. Coordination with the army surgeon was required to ensure that additional hospital units were available to leapfrog over one another as the supported divisions advanced. One problem encountered with the field hospitals during the rapid advances from the Roer to the Rhine was that not all the hospitalization units of the field hospital could be moved simultaneously on organic transportation assets, so vehicles had to be provided by other medical units to assist their moves.[89]

Coordination with the evacuation hospitals was more complex, since they were not under the control of the groups that evacuated patients to them. Patient flow into the hospitals was controlled by placing a hospital in support of (but not under the control of) one of the groups. In the event that a hospital could not be placed in support of only one group, bed credits were issued to each supported group. A bed credit was a bed in a hospital dedicated to the support of one unit. As patients filled beds, the beds available to the group decreased, and increased again as patients were discharged, died, or transferred to another facility. In theory, when all the beds in a hospital dedicated to support a group were filled, a group sent its patients to another hospital. In units subordinate to the 1st Medical Group, evacuation was controlled using evacuation ratios; units would send patients to one facility in direct proportion to the number sent to another facility—the proportion (or ratio) being specified by the group headquarters. The ratio appears to have been selected based on the tactical situation and the beds available in supporting hospitals and was changed as frequently as the situation dictated to avoid overtaxing the supporting medical facilities. While the unit journals of the 1st Medical Group and its subordinate units show how the system was used within the group, it is not known if this system was in use throughout the Ninth Army or if it was unique to the 1st Medical Group.[90]

As might be expected, this system worked well when patient admission rates were low, but it had to be monitored very carefully as patient admission rates increased. During periods of heavy combat, the system tended to break down almost completely, as the surgical backlog became the dominant factor over beds available in deciding which facilities could accept patients.[91] Surgical backlog is defined as the period, generally measured in hours, between the time a patient is delivered to a facility and the time that patient enters an operating room. Obviously, with a fixed number of operating tables in a hospital, if patients arrive at a facility faster than surgery can be completed, the surgical backlog will increase. The situation, in fact, prompted the author of the group's after-action report for February 1945 (written shortly after the Roer River crossing) to comment:

> In present and previous operations, bed status of Evac Hospitals never approached capacity; but surgical backlog required constant checking by Group that patients might be dispatched to the quickest available surgery. For this reason, Group CP's should be as far forward as wire communications with Evacuation Hospitals will permit; because adjustment of flow must be made at the source (Division Clearing Elements) by personal contact. Furthermore, constant personal contact should be maintained with Div Clr Elms to anticipate and regulate casualty flow during periods of great activity.[92]

The 1st Medical Group also found that the hospitals supporting them (again, not under Colonel Veigel's command or control) often used different methods of computing surgical backlog—an administrative matter which may have affected patient care. As the group noted after the Roer River crossing:

> If one hospital includes shock treatment and x-ray in its backlog, it may claim a greater backlog than another hospital which does not include these factors but which actually has more surgery to perform. This situation makes a difference to the wounded man; because Group

> sends him where lowest backlog is claimed; and, in the case cited, he may have to wait longer for treatment than if bothe [sic] hospitals used identical systems of computation.

> Take, for example, a recent situation: A hospital called Group and announced a twenty-four hour backlog. Group immediately shifted evacuation to hospitals having about twelve hours. An officer was sent to investigate, however; and in forty-five minutes he discovered that the hospital in question actually had reduced its surgery to eight hours—a reduction of sixteen hours in forty-five minutes! Meanwhile the wounded had been routed to hospitals having twelve hours and had lost four hours prior to time of surgical treatment.[93]

While it is impossible to attribute deaths in hospitals directly to surgical backlog, it should be intuitively obvious that a delay in sending a wounded soldier into surgery would increase patient morbidity and mortality. The problem in the 1st Medical Group appeared to have been caused by how the hospital staffs computed surgical backlog, which, as can be seen by this example, can have a significant impact on how long a patient waits before entering surgery. After the Roer crossing, the group recommended that "surgical backlog should be expressed in terms of total patient operating hours divided by the number of operating tables in use."[94]

By the morning of 23 February, the day the attack was scheduled to start, the 1st Medical Group was still composed of two medical battalions, the 183d and 430th. A third, the 188th Medical Battalion, joined the group on the 24th, the day following the start of the attack (see figure 2).[95] At 0245 on 23 February, the fires of over 1,000 pieces of artillery announced to the Germans that the long-awaited assault was about to begin.[96] Despite the anticipated problems encountered in getting assault bridges across the turbulent river and in moving follow-up forces while under enemy fire, the initial assaults went well, and by the end of the first day, all four of the assaulting divisions had advanced several miles inland. While strong defensive positions had been prepared by the Germans, many of the German troops who were to man them had been diverted to defend against the Canadian First Army, which had launched an offensive of its own on 8 February 1945.[97] By 25 February, the U.S Ninth Army had consolidated the divisional bridgeheads and had made contact with the VII Corps to the south.[98] General Simpson ordered a breakthrough attempt, and enemy defenses continued to crumble. The XIII Corps bypassed München-Gladbach and by 3 March had reached Krefeld and the banks of the Rhine.[99]

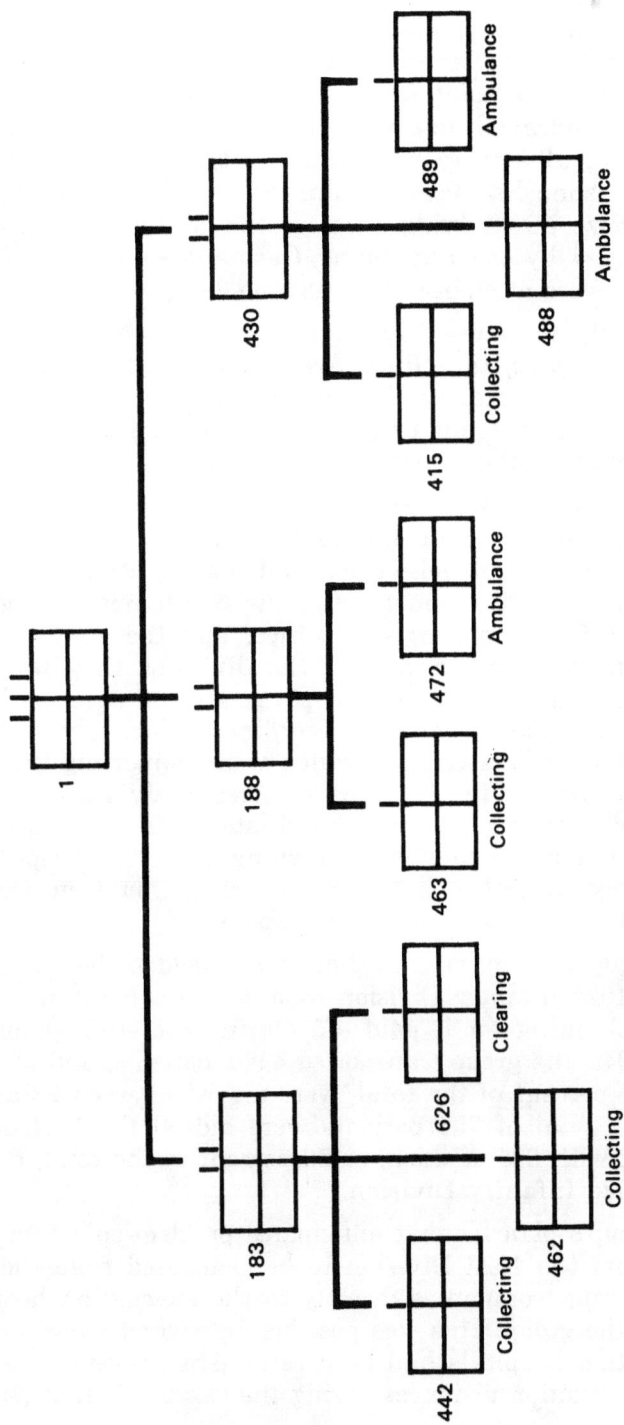

Figure 2. Task organization, 1st Medical Group, 1 March 1945

München-Gladbach, which it was feared would be fiercely defended by the enemy, was captured by a single regiment on 1 March, the largest German metropolitan area to be captured in the west to that point in the war.[100] The enemy attempted an orderly withdrawal across bridges at Wesel and Rheinberg. By 11 March, all enemy resistance west of the Rhine in the Ninth Army zone had been eliminated, but despite several attempts to seize intact bridges across the Rhine River, all had been destroyed by the advancing Germans—one while Ninth Army forces were attempting to cross it.[101]

By rapidly maneuvering against enemy weaknesses and exploiting successes, the Ninth Army now stood on the banks of the Rhine, historically the last defense of Germany from enemies in the west. Plans progressed rapidly to effect a crossing and the capture of the Ruhr industrial region beyond.

While the 1st Medical Group did not issue extensive written operations plans, it by no means operated in a vacuum. The group commander, Colonel Veigel, and his S3, Major Prideaux, made frequent coordination trips to the Ninth Army Surgeon's office, the XIII Corps Surgeon's office, and the surgeons and medical battalion commanders of the divisions they would be supporting to ensure that all their plans were in agreement and mutually supporting. They also coordinated laterally with the 30th and 31st Medical Groups, which were supporting the other corps of the army. Finally, they met frequently with the commanders and staffs of their subordinate units to ensure that they knew the plans and were carrying them out properly. If they had any control over the matter, they would ensure that there would be few surprises in this operation.[102]

The group had anticipated that there would be heavy casualties in the 102d Infantry Division zone during the initial assault, and their planning for it paid off. During the entire month of February 1945, the group transported 4,951 patients, and of these, 3,296, or 67 percent of the total, were moved between 23 and 28 February. A total of 704 patients were moved the first day of the assault, with 395 of them, or 56 percent of the total, coming from the 102d Infantry Division.[103]

The group's plan for that anticipated problem called for some patients from the 102d Division to be evacuated from the division's collecting companies directly to the evacuation hospitals supporting the group. This was possible for several reasons. First, the evacuation hospitals had been established close to the Roer to reduce evacuation distances during the assault so that patients only had to be evacuated about fourteen miles from the collecting companies. Second, the roads were in good condition, so patients could be moved quickly to the evacuation hospitals—the average evacuation time being less than thirty minutes from the time a patient left the collecting company until he arrived at an evacuation hospital. Finally, less severely injured patients could be evacuated to the 327th Medical Battalion's clearing station for treatment, and the more severely injured would be stabilized at the clearing station before further movement to the evacuation hospitals. All in all, 120 patients were evacuated directly from the collecting companies, while another 275 were evacuated from the divisional clearing company—most in the first 8 hours of the assault.[104]

This plan had several immediately apparent advantages. First, it reduced the number of patients passing through the clearing company, preventing degradation of patient care there. Second, since the thirty ambulances of the 498th Motor Ambulance Company were added to those of the division—normally the only assets evacuating the collecting companies—patients were evacuated quickly from the collecting stations, preventing those facilities from becoming overloaded, thus allowing them to provide a higher quality of care. And finally, as already mentioned, this allowed the most seriously injured patients to be seen at an evacuation hospital within thirty minutes after leaving the collecting companies.[105] Similar reasons are given today when discussing the use of air ambulances to move patients directly from the site of injury to the hospital best suited to provide them treatment, thus bypassing facilities in the normal chain of evacuation.

This system would not have worked without proper control of the ambulances providing evacuation. To provide this control, the 430th Medical Battalion established an ambulance regulation point behind the 102d Infantry Division. This control point was in telephonic contact with the group headquarters, which allowed the group to change the evacuation ratios rapidly as bed spaces decreased and surgical backlog increased in the evacuation hospitals supporting the group.[106]

Fortunately, the 1st Medical Group had made plans to control patient flow, for the surgical backlog at the hospitals increased rapidly. By 1100 on the 23d, the 91st Evacuation Hospital was reporting a surgical backlog of six hours, having admitted "approximately 77" patients. By 1300, the 41st Evacuation Hospital was reporting a backlog of eighteen hours.[107] This continued throughout the night, and by 1300 on 24 February, the 100th Evacuation Hospital reported that its surgical backlog had increased from two hours to nine hours in the short period between 1700 and 1800 and by 2015 was reporting a surgical backlog of eighty patients and fifteen hours.[108] This problem with surgical backlog appears to have been much more serious than had been anticipated by the group before the operation, as they commented extensively on it in their monthly after-action report.[109] The medical situation in the 102d Infantry Division improved after the army's engineers installed bridges at Linnich and armored forces could be committed to the bridgehead.[110] The bridges allowed ambulances to proceed across the river to pick up patients, while the commitment of armored forces started a breakout that in turn led to lower casualty rates.

During the advance from the Roer to the Rhine, the rapidly changing situation, as the troops continually moved forward, required frequent moves on the part of the medical units supporting the maneuver forces, including command and control elements. The 1st Medical Group headquarters moved four times during the advance: on 27 February to Beggendorf, Germany; on 1 March to Rurich, Germany, on the east side of the Roer; on 2 March to Hardt, Germany; and on 4 March to Viersen, Germany.[111] In all cases, the headquarters established itself in

Courtesy of Thomas S. Prideaux

The 1st Medical Group's command post, Hardt, Germany, 2—4 March 1945

The Roer River crossing site at Linnich

fixed facilities, although some were heavily damaged and required some repair before being occupied.[112]

While the group sent out advance parties and then moved its headquarters as a whole, the 430th Medical Battalion took a different approach to the requirement for rapid movement: it split its headquarters into two echelons. The forward section contained the commander, most of the S3 section, and the battalion message center, while the rear echelon was composed of the remainder of the headquarters. The forward section could be ready to displace in a matter of minutes and functioned well as an ambulance regulating point or liaison team, often, in fact, collocating with the clearing company of one of its supported divisions. The rear echelon, on the other hand, could move at a more leisurely pace, allowing it to select better sites for the battalion command post, which the forward echelon would rejoin once a crisis had passed. Like the 1st Medical Group headquarters, the battalion headquarters of the 430th moved four times during the advance from the Roer,[113] while the 188th Medical Battalion headquarters moved five times between 27 February and 10 March 1945.[114] The 183d Medical Battalion, with its mission to provide support to army units in the 1st Medical Group's zone rather than to committed divisions, moved only once, on 10 March 1945.[115]

After the initial crossings on 23 February, activities within the units of the group returned to a normal, if somewhat hectic, pace. The group found that, as the pace of the advance increased due to the crumbling German resistance, the number of casualties requiring evacuation decreased, while the distance each individual casualty had to travel increased. This caused total patient-miles traveled to remain constant. Thus, while individual patients traveled farther—potentially increasing patient morbidity—the smaller number of patients meant that the total number of miles traveled by the ambulances of the group, as a whole, remained about the same. The group also found that the best way to manage hospitalization assets was to try to keep the surgical backlog and the number of beds occupied as constant as possible among the hospitals to which they evacuated. This kept the staff at any one facility from being overloaded (if at all possible). The group found that field hospital units, when employed to support divisions moving on the same axis of advance, were best utilized when centrally located, rather than when placed in direct support of any one division.[116]

One other entry the group made in their after-action report concerned the use of collecting companies. The 1st Medical Group discovered that while clearing companies and ambulance companies were employed in platoons or sections, the collecting com-

Wounded being evacuated in a half-track by medics in Germany (World War II)

pany was often employed in piecemeal fashion. To quote from the group's after-action report:

> As part of the army medical service, separate collecting companies are often scattered to the four winds with the litter platoon reinforcing an evacuation hospital, the station platoon running dispensaries or aid stations, and the ambulance platoon committed piecemeal over a wide area. In this connection the following principle should be set down: Collecting companies should be used, where possible, as a single element or in as large an element as possible to ship [toward the front?] [.] [The advantages to this] are immeasurable; greatest advantage should be taken of such tactical situations as river-crossings or attacks of fortified positions to utilize separate collecting companies *as units* in augmenting corps and division medical service.[117]

For example, during the period 9—28 February, the 442d Medical Collecting Company (attached to the 183d Medical Battalion) was employed as follows. First, the company headquarters was established in Valkenburg, Holland. One Medical Corps officer and three enlisted men operated an aid station near the town. The rest of the station platoon, the litter-bearer platoon, and two ambulances from the ambulance platoon supported the 91st Evacuation Hospital; three ambulances supported one of the clearing platoons of the 626th Medical Clearing Company; two ambulances supported the 111th Evacuation Hospital; one ambulance supported an aid station near Heerlen; one ambulance supported an aid station near Valkenburg; and the last ambulance supported an aid station of the 36th Reinforcement Battalion.[118] While the support to the 91st Evacuation Hospital was not defined, it probably meant that the enlisted men of the 442d were used to provide additional staffing on the wards of the hospital.

While the XIII and XVI Corps were advancing to the Rhine, their axes of advance crossed one another. In order to simplify support relationships and to avoid moving many supporting medical units, the Ninth Army Surgeon directed that the medical groups supporting the two corps would exchange missions, so on 9 March 1945, the 1st Medical Group assumed the support of XVI Corps, while the 30th Medical Group, which had been supporting the XVI Corps, assumed the mission of supporting XIII Corps.[119] The transition went smoothly, even to the extent that Colonel Veigel took the commander of the 30th Medical Group to meet the surgeons of the various units the 30th Medical Group would now be supporting.[120]

Maj. Gen. Alvan C. Gillem, Jr., commander of U.S. XIII Corps

Maj. Gen. John B. Anderson, commander of U.S. XVI Corps

This new mission required the 1st Medical Group headquarters, as well as several of its subordinate units, to move
again to provide better control over units in its new zone of
operations. The group moved to Brockhuysen, Germany, on 9
March. The site it chose, however, was in an area being turned
over to the British Second Army, so the 1st Medical Group headquarters moved to Aldenkirk, Germany, the next day (allegedly
at the request of Field Marshal Montgomery of the British forces).
On the 19th, the headquarters moved again, this time to Lintfort,
Germany, "in order to be better situated tactically for the con-
templated RHINE RIVER crossing."[121]

While waiting for forces to be assembled for the assault crossing of the Rhine, the 1st Medical Group put its time to good
use refining plans and ensuring that the units it now supported,
as well as the hospitals supporting the group, understood and
would adhere to its plans.[122] Meanwhile, subordinate units refined
their supporting plans and ensured that necessary maintenance
was performed. They also conducted chemical warfare refresher
training—not because they feared that the Germans would use
chemicals but because Allied artillery and air attacks might
release dangerous industrial chemicals stockpiled in the Ruhr
industrial area.[123]

This is the first mention of chemical-defense preparations
in the records of the 1st Medical Group since it had departed
for France aboard the *Mount Vernon*—and even then the men's
primary concern was whether their impermeable uniforms (pro-
tected against chemicals) had to be carried in their backpacks,
their duffel bags, or their footlockers.[124]

The crossing of the Roer had been the first major operation
for the 1st Medical Group, and despite all their years of training
in the United States, they were not quite ready for it. It was,
in the words of one member of the unit, "sorta 'touch and go'
but not as bad as some had it."[125] But the staff learned quickly
from their mistakes (most noticeably the problems encountered
with surgical backlog) and prepared to ensure that similar problems did not occur during the next river crossing. Soon, the
Rhine River would be crossed, and the war in Europe would
near its end.

III. THE RHINE RIVER CROSSING

Once the Roer River had been crossed, there remained only one real barrier between the Allied armies in the west and the heart of Germany: the Rhine River. For hundreds of years, the Rhine had been recognized by the German people as their final protective barrier against invasion from the west. In the summer of 1944, following the Normandy invasion, the German commanders in the west had repeatedly asked Hitler's permission to withdraw behind the Rhine. This, they felt, was their only hope of stopping the Allied advance. Hitler repeatedly refused, ordering his commanders to contest every inch of ground in front of the Allies. Thus, by the time the Germans abandoned the western bank of the Rhine in March of 1945, the force that might have been able to prevent an Allied crossing of the river had been crippled: mauled on the beaches, decimated in the withdrawal through France, and crushed in the last, desperate battle of the Ardennes. While the forces opposing the U.S. Ninth Army on the Rhine were still formidable, they were not as powerful as they would have been had the Germans withdrawn to the Rhine earlier.[126]

General Eisenhower and his staff had decided early in the planning for the invasion of Europe that the main effort in the Rhine River crossing would be in the north, in the 21st Army Group zone. They had two reasons for doing so. First, although later rendered less significant by the Yalta Conference's agreement on the limits of the Allied advance into Germany, a crossing in the northern sector would leave the Allies in the west much better situated for a final drive to the German capital, Berlin, than would crossings in either the central or southern sectors of the front. Second, and perhaps of greater operational significance, was that a crossing in the north would lead to the capture of the great German industrial region along the Ruhr River. This region, extending for fifty miles along the eastern bank of the Rhine and sixty miles to the east on both sides of the Ruhr, produced 65 percent of the steel and 56 percent of the coal used in Germany before the war. Additionally, with the fall of the Saar industrial region to the Americans farther south and Silesia to the Russians, the Ruhr was the only major source of electrical power for Germany. A crossing of the Rhine in the north, with the subsequent reduction of the Ruhr, would all but ensure a rapid Allied victory.[127]

The Ninth Army plan called for the XVI Corps to make an assault crossing at Rheinberg. Once this bridgehead was enlarged sufficiently, the XIX Corps would also be committed east of the Rhine. The XIII Corps would continue to secure the west bank of the Rhine. After being relieved of its mission to secure the west bank by the Fifteenth Army, which was acting as an army of occupation behind the Ninth Army, the XIII Corps would join the XVI and XIX Corps west of the Rhine. Once across the river, the army would drive east toward the industrial city of Hamm, and from there to the Elbe River. The XVI Corps, after securing the initial bridgehead, would wheel south to link up with the First Army, encircling the Ruhr industrial region.[128]

The XVI Corps' plan called for two infantry divisions, the 30th and 79th, to cross the river simultaneously at Mehrum and Milchplatz. After the bridgehead was expanded, the 35th and 75th Infantry Divisions would be committed (see map 2). The 8th Armored Division, as the corps reserve, would be held west of the Rhine until the battle for the far shore was developed enough to show where it could be employed best.[129]

In order to achieve tactical surprise, the army implemented a deception plan during the buildup of forces on the west bank of the Rhine. Medical units were not excluded from this plan, and all units were required to remove red crosses from vehicles and equipment. Ambulances moved in ones and twos, by infiltration rather than in convoys and, when not in use, were kept under overhead cover. In order to make the Germans believe that the XVI Corps' main effort would be in the southern portion of the army zone, a medical clearing company was set up across the river from Duisburg and provided with extra tentage. Ambulance traffic was continued to and from the facility to make it appear as though the unit was still engaged in its medical-support mission.[130] On at least one occasion, the 1st Medical Group's S3 flew over the group's area to observe how well camouflage was being maintained and to report to the group's subordinate units on its effectiveness.[131] Of course, once the attack commenced, the requirement for camouflaging medical facilities came to an end.[132]

By 24 March 1945, the day the attack began, the 1st Medical Group was composed of the 20th Field Hospital and two medical battalions, the 188th and 430th. The group's third medical battalion, the 183d, had been removed from the group on 15 March 1945[133] to provide medical support to the XVIII Airborne Corps under the direct control of the Ninth Army Surgeon's office (see figure 3).[134]

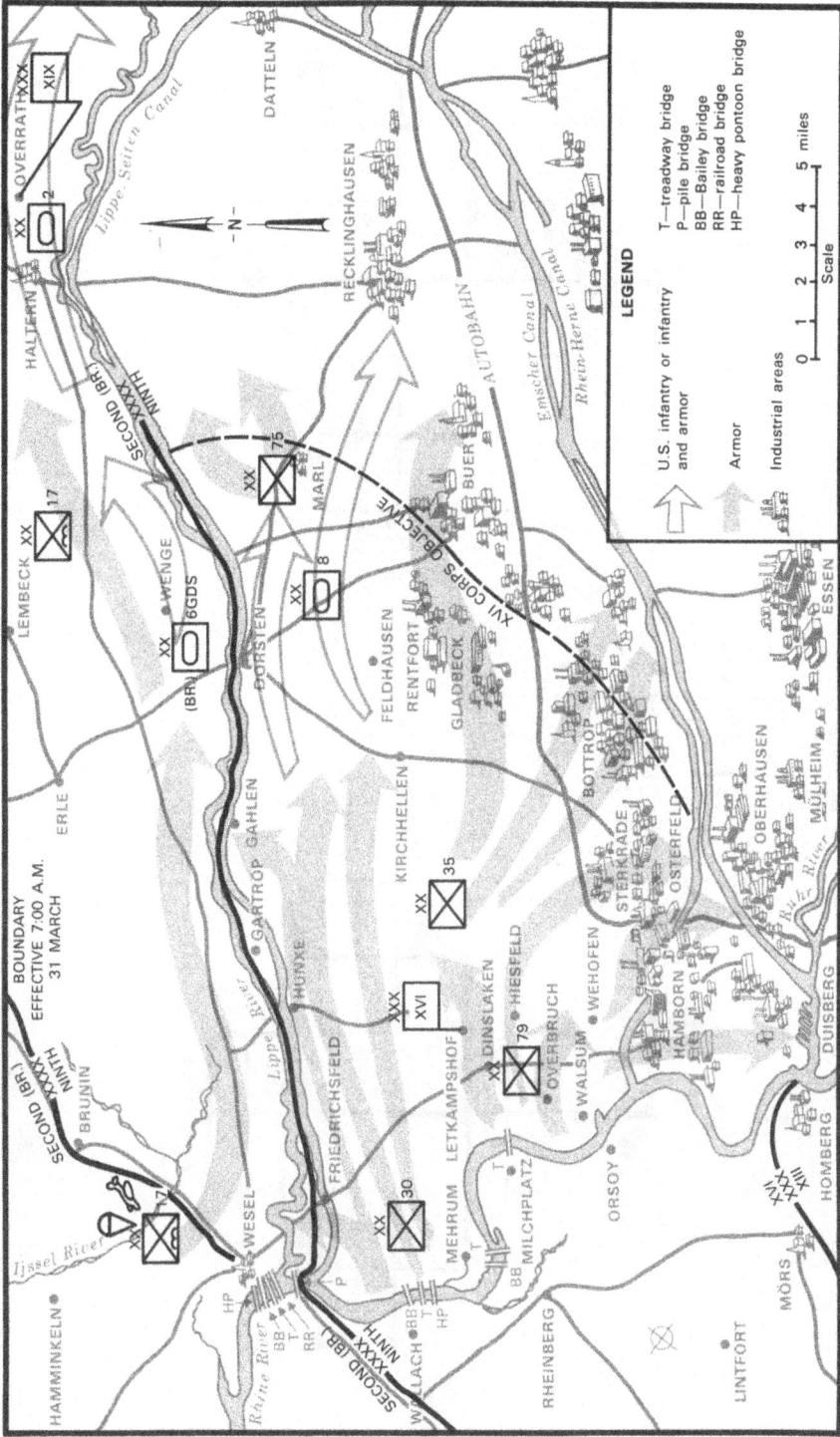

LEGEND

U.S. infantry or infantry and armor

Armor

Industrial areas

T—treadway bridge
P—pile bridge
BB—Bailey bridge
RR—railroad bridge
HP—heavy pontoon bridge

Scale
0 1 2 3 4 5 miles

Map 2. The expansion beyond the Rhine bridgehead

44

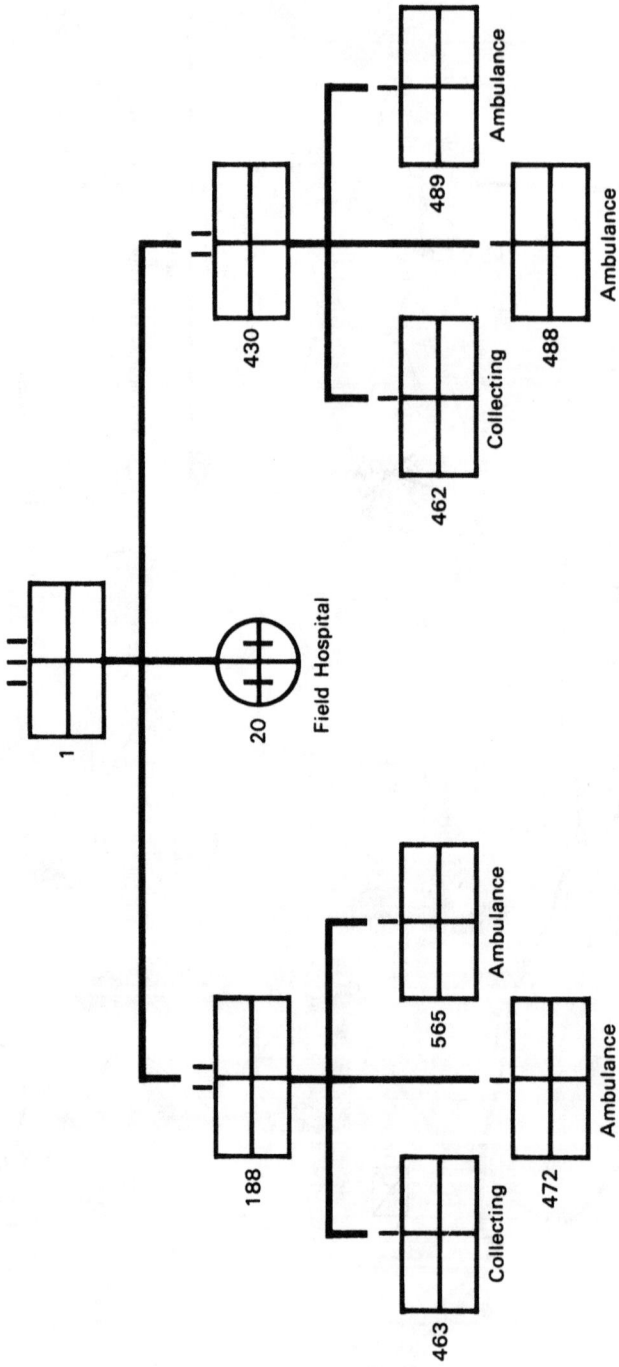

Figure 3. Task organization, 1st Medical Group, 24 March 1945

While doctrine called for the supporting medical group to reinforce divisions of the corps while the corps' attached medical battalion provided care for corps troops in the rear area, the XVI Corps Surgeon, Colonel Harold L. Furlong, adopted a different concept for the actual crossing. Under his plan, he suggested

> reinforcement of division medical service from corps medical battalion, using special equipment on near and far shore and on the water, with reinforcement of corps medical battalion from Army to insure rapid evacuation of casualties from across the river, and conservation of critical medical supplies and personnel for more advantageous use later.[135]

This plan covered only the initial assault crossings and the establishment of the bridgehead, after which the corps would return to a doctrinal support concept.

This plan, Furlong and his staff believed, offered a number of advantages over the other options that they considered. It made maximum use of divisional and corps medical personnel while ensuring that the medical treatment facilities provided by the corps would allow continuous support by leapfrogging second-echelon facilities past each other as the supported divisions began their advance from the far shore. The one disadvantage they saw in the plan—that corps and army personnel on the near shore would be mixed and that army and corps medical-treatment facilities would both be providing care to corps troops—could "readily be overcome by careful coordination and command and control."[136]

At 0200 on 24 March 1945, the 30th Infantry Division began its assault across the Rhine following a massive one-hour barrage from the collected artillery of all three corps of the Ninth Army. An hour later, following another hour-long artillery barrage, the 79th Infantry Division began its crossing farther to the south in the corps' sector. The British had also begun their crossings at 0200, and at 1000, the XVIII Corps conducted an airborne assault. Resistance was initially light but increased as the forces of the corps moved inland. Nonetheless, by 25 March, the corps was twenty-four to forty-eight hours ahead of schedule in its advance.[137] While the capture of a partially intact bridge at Remagen in the First Army zone on 7 March meant that the Ninth Army would not be the first American army across the Rhine, General Eisenhower decided to stay with his original plan to place the main effort of the Allies in the 21st Army Group's zone. While the First Army was getting all the publicity in the

U.S. troops crossing the Rhine under fire

stateside press, the Ninth Army was bringing the war that much closer to its conclusion.[138] By 26 March, the 35th Infantry Division had crossed the Rhine and was assembling on the eastern shore, while the XIII Corps assumed control of the west bank of the river and the XIX Corps prepared to be committed to the east.[139] By the 29th, the 8th Armored Division cleared Dortsten and Feldhausen, while the 35th Infantry Division cleared the city of Gladbach, and the 79th Infantry Division advanced to within a mile of the Rhein-Herne Canal.[140]

On 30 March, the corps continued to advance, clearing the towns of Rurhassel, Polsum, Bottrop, and Buer. The north bank of the Rhein-Herne Canal was reached. Meanwhile, the XIX Corps launched its first attack east of the Rhine. On the 31st, the 2d Armored Division achieved a breakthrough in the XIX Corps' zone and advanced thirty-five miles, while the XVI Corps cleared more of the banks of the Rhein-Herne Canal.[141] The end was now only a matter of time.

Although the 1st Medical Group would have preferred to place its hospital units along a single axis where they could support both divisions, the distance between the two division axes prevented this. Therefore, the 1st placed a hospital unit in support of each division, with a third held in reserve. It did this because it expected a greater number of casualties than in the Roer crossing and because of the limited objectives of the assault. When the first clearing company from the 30th Medical Battalion established itself on the east bank of the Rhine, the group established a hospital unit of the 48th Field Hospital in support of it, where it received the corps' first nontransportable patients.[142] To assist in the treatment of these patients, two auxiliary surgical teams and two shock teams were attached to the 1st Medical Group from the 5th Auxiliary Surgical Group and were further attached by the group to the field hospitals.[143] As the divisional clearing companies moved forward, the hospital units of the 20th Field Hospital were left in place and were replaced with hospital units of the 48th Field Hospital, while those of the 20th reverted to field army control.[144] The army had placed five evacuation hospitals—the 100th, 105th, 108th, 111th, and 119th—in support of the XVI Corps (and the 1st Medical Group) at the start of the assault, while another evacuation hospital, the 91st, was loaded on its vehicles and prepared to displace forward, which it did on 30 March, establishing itself in the vicinity of Vorde, on the east bank of the Rhine.[145]

In the 430th Medical Battalion, the 488th Motor Ambulance Company provided evacuation for the 79th Infantry Division,

Courtesy of Thomas S. Prideaux

The Ludendorff railroad bridge (called the Remagen bridge) across the Rhine River, a lucky acquisition from the Germans

The 1st Medical Group crossing the Rhine River, May 1945

while the 489th Motor Ambulance Company evacuated the 35th Division and various corps units. The 462d Medical Collecting Company was one of the units providing support to corps units and was responsible for providing collecting support to engineer units constructing bridges in the northern portion of the corps' zone. While the litter-bearer platoon provided aidmen at the bridging sites and the collecting station platoon established their collecting stations nearby, the ambulance platoon provided evacuation support to various engineer, artillery, and antiaircraft artillery units in the area. The 430th Medical Battalion's fourth company, the 415th Medical Collecting Company, was established at Repelen, Germany, to serve as a holding area for casualties should the need arise, while its litter-bearer platoon augmented the 79th Infantry Division during the initial crossing.[146] Units of the 183d Medical Battalion provided similar services to engineer units, probably in the southern portion of the corps' zone.[147]

The assault crossings of the Rhine River went much easier for the 1st Medical Group than did the crossing of the Roer a few weeks earlier. There appear to be several reasons for this. First, the massive preassault artillery barrage, the deception plan, and the rapidly crumbling German defenses all helped to produce fewer casualties than had been anticipated. Moreover, hospitals were placed closer to the river line, and more important, the group was initially supported by five semimobile evacuation hospitals—with a total of 2,000 beds—rather than the three hospitals and 1,200 beds it had shared with the 30th Medical Group during the Roer crossings. But most important, the group had used the Roer crossings as what physicians call "a good teaching case." Like all good soldiers, the 1st Medical Group had learned from its mistakes and implemented procedures— most notably a standard method of calculating surgical backlog—in cooperation with its supported and supporting units. With the greater number of hospitals, coupled with standardized procedures, surgical backlog became so minimal as to escape comment in the group's unit journal—a vastly different situation than that following the Roer crossing.[148]

On 26 March, the 430th Medical Battalion moved to Rheinberg to establish an ambulance control point but found that the need that had required one the previous month did not exist, so it was discontinued. On 29 March, the battalion crossed the Rhine and established its headquarters in Stockum, Germany. The battalion moved again before the end of the month, this time to Dinslakenerbruck to better support the corps' turn to the south to encircle the Ruhr.[149] On 28 March, the group headquarters crossed the Rhine, setting up in Letkampshof, where it would remain until 6 April 1945.[150]

IV. THE REST OF THE STORY

By mid-April, the war was all but over for the XVI Corps, if not for the 1st Medical Group. On 12 April, the 2d Armored Division of the XIX Corps established a bridgehead over the Elbe River, followed a day later with a second bridgehead by the 83d Infantry Division. In the XVI Corps, Duisburg was taken on 13 April, and by the 14th, the corps had eliminated all resistance in its zone of the Ruhr pocket. On the 17th, the Ruhr pocket was completely eliminated as the First Army cleared its zone of the pocket. While the XIII and XIX Corps continued to clear their zones, the XVI Corps turned its attention to occupation duties. On 30 April, the XIX Corps' 113th Cavalry Group made contact with Russian forces advancing toward the Elbe. Finally, on 7 May 1945, the Germans surrendered to the Allied High Command. The war in Europe would end on 8 May 1945.[151]

The 1st Medical Group's mission changed in the month of April from that of providing third-echelon medical support to the XVI Corps to "supervising and operating hospitals for PWs [prisoners of war], liberated allied PWs, and for Displaced persons of allied nations."[152] Colonel Veigel had anticipated this mission early in his planning and had alerted his subordinate commanders to watch carefully for overrun PW camps and hospitals.[153] This warning paid off; on 1 April 1945, an ambulance platoon leader from the 430th Medical Battalion reported that the 35th Infantry Division had overrun a German general hospital. The 430th Medical Battalion's S2 and S3 investigated the hospital and found it contained German military patients and civilian patients of several nationalities but no Allied patients.[154] The procedures for the control of "uncovered"* German military hospitals, published that same day by the Ninth Army Surgeon's Office, directed that each medical group place the responsibility for all uncovered German military hospitals in its zone under the supervision of one of its subordinate medical battalion commanders.[155] This mission was assigned to the 430th Medical Battalion by the 1st Medical Group headquarters. At the same time, the 430th was relieved of its tactical support mission.[156]

---

*The term "uncovered" was used by Ninth Army's medical personnel to mean discovered.

U.S. infantrymen aboard an armored car on the way to the Elbe

Following the discovery of the first German hospital, several more were rapidly uncovered in Ahlen, Munster, "Gr. Reckum" [sic], Velen, and Coesfeld. These uncovered hospitals operated a total of 5,409 beds; the battalion operated an additional 700 beds in a hospital for displaced persons in Recklinghausen. To supervise the operation of the hospitals, the battalion used portions of the 415th, 462d, and 481st Medical Collecting Companies and the 666th Medical Clearing Company; the displaced persons hospital was operated by the 95th Medical Gas Treatment Battalion, which had been placed under the operational control of the 430th Medical Battalion.[157]

When the Ruhr pocket was reduced in mid-April, the tactical medical support mission for the 1st Medical Group came to an end. The group and its subordinate elements had transported 6,063 patients between various medical facilities in the XVI Corps area,[158] but now, the real work of the month was beginning. All elements of the group turned their attention to the care of patients found in uncovered hospitals. By 30 April, the group was caring for 34,116 PWs, 3,294 liberated Allied PWs, and 972 German civilians—a total of 39,404 patients.[159] The 1st Medical Group was simultaneously reorganizing these facilities to provide an additional 11,200 beds for patients still being uncovered.[160]

To provide this care, the 1st Medical Group had available to it the 48th Field Hospital and three medical battalions—the 183d, 185th, and 430th.[161] The total strength of the group was 92 officers, 18 nurses, and 984 enlisted men. An additional 365 officers, 1,112 nurses, and 1,228 enlisted personnel were available from "not US" sources—presumably captured German military and civilian medical personnel (see figure 4).[162]

But what level of care do these numbers equate to? According to the group's after-action report, if care were provided to U.S. standards, 99 semimobile (400-bed) evacuation hospitals would be required, with a total staff of 29,205. The staff available to the 1st Medical Group amounted to 13 percent of that number. Further problems were caused by the need to segregate patients into proper categories and to ensure that Allied patients were given the level of care that they required—which was often far higher than that provided by the Germans before the facilities came under the control of the U.S. Ninth Army.[163]

One example (perhaps, an extreme case) from the 430th Medical Battalion serves to illustrate the problems encountered by the 1st Medical Group in supporting its new mission. Stalag VI, a German PW camp holding 24,000 Russian prisoners, was uncovered in Hemer, Germany. Of the prisoners, 8,000 required hospitalization, half of them for tuberculosis. The battalion had no available hospitalization facilities, yet it needed to get the

Russians under medical supervision quickly, for they were dying at a rate in excess of sixty per day. Fortunately, the battalion had at its disposal a substantial number of German medical personnel, and the 75th Infantry Division was able to make available a former German barracks in its area which, though bomb damaged, would make an adequate hospital facility. The German staff and captured medical supplies were moved into the facility, American cots and blankets were added, and a 3,000-bed hospital was operational within 48 hours. Some PW facilities were overloaded to clear beds in several other facilities, and care was quickly provided to the Russians. The next problem the 430th Medical Battalion encountered, which was eventually resolved, was language difficulties, as it was difficult to convince the Russians that they would now be treated to American standards, if possible, rather than the level of care the Germans had provided to them in the past.[164]

The 1st Medical Group continued its mission throughout the month of May. The greatest problem for the group was sorting patients by nationality and status and segregating them into hospitals based on those criteria. Allied patients also had to be transported to better facilities than those in which the Germans had been treating them. By 11 May, the group had finished the sorting process, having reached a census of 48,531 patients in 149 facilities.[165] The 1st Medical Group found the Germans used to staff the facilities to be, in general, cooperative. Two areas were occasionally troublesome but were, for the most part, easily corrected. First, the German medical personnel tended to leave German PW patients in facilities longer than they should rather than transfer them to Allied PW camps. Second, the Germans sometimes tended not to provide as high a level of care for Allied patients as had been directed. Both of these problems were easily corrected with proper supervision.[166]

Supply was an additional problem. As might be expected, supplying all these facilities was a massive job, and between 15 and 27 May 1945, the 1st Medical Group distributed, among other items, 9,000 blankets; 3,000 cots; 5,000 pants, shirts, drawers, and pajamas; 110 gallons of DDT; 6,539 pounds of chlorinated lime; 57,500 pounds of laundry soap; and 17,350 rolls of toilet paper.[167] Class I supply was on a similar scale, and difficulties were expected in drawing rations for such large numbers.[168] The personnel of the group were also spread thin among the facilities. Since the Ninth Army required that an American be placed in command of each facility, the large

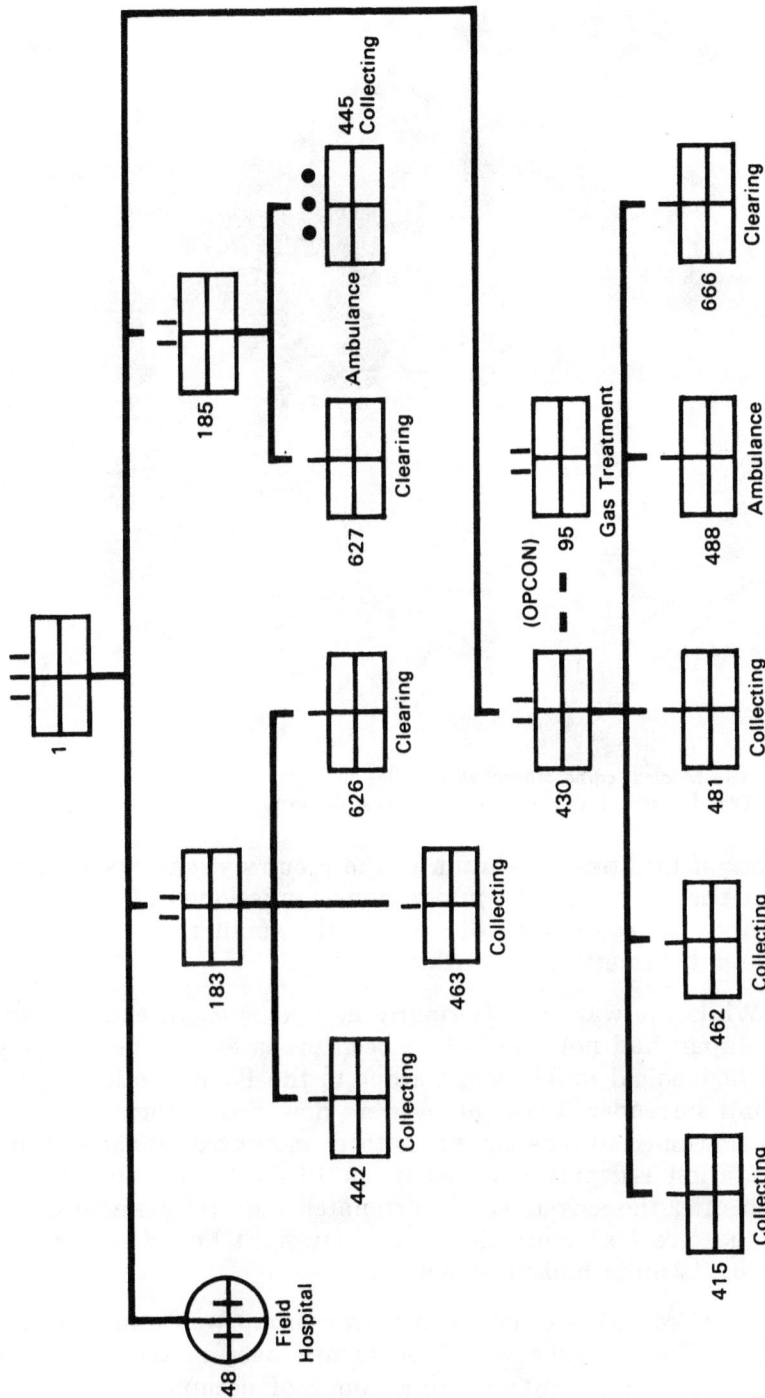

Figure 4. Task organization, 1st Medical Group, 1 May 1945

The Medical corps stockpiled supplies in huge concentrations during World War II (example, Naples Medical Center)

number of facilities in relation to the group's strength sometimes meant that a private or junior noncommissioned officer would be placed in "command" of some of the smaller facilities, often as the only American present.[169]

While the war with Germany had come to an end, the war with Japan had not. Plans had been prepared for the redeployment of medical units from Europe to the Pacific following the German surrender. These plans were now accelerated, and some units scheduled to redeploy up to three months after the German capitulation redeployed as early as 10 June 1945—barely one month after the surrender.[170] Fortunately, the 1st Medical Group headquarters had more than the forty-eight hours' notice that some of its units had to redeploy.

On 24 May 1945, the 1st Medical Group was informed that the XVI Corps sector would be turned over to the British as part of the agreement covering zones of occupation.[171] On 28

May, the group headquarters was relieved of its attachments, entered an inactive status, and began to prepare for overseas movement.[172] By that date, the group's patient census had declined from its high of 48,531 to 36,000.[173] On 7 June, the group headquarters, accompanied by the 472d, 488th, and 489th Motor Ambulance Companies, departed for Camp Twenty Grand, a redeployment staging area outside the port of Le Havre, France,[174] arriving there on 11 June.[175] Staging at Camp Twenty Grand, the group boarded the Army transport *Sea Owl* (a liberty ship much like the countless others sailing the globe at that time) at noon on 17 June.[176] On the 18th, they left the ship, which could not sail due to engine problems (noted the war diary, "Morale: rather low").[177] Four days later, the group again boarded the *Sea Owl*, and this time they successfully left port ("Morale: excellent").[178]

Eight days later, the detachment arrived at Camp Shanks, New York, where it was assigned to the Second Army.[179] While

Courtesy of Harry L. Gans (Col., USA, ret.)

Members of Headquarters Detachment, 1st Medical Group: left to right in front row—Cpl. J. I. Kitchens, Pfc. Hartman, Cpl. Altman, Pfc. Dambra, Sgt. Malcolm D. Blankenship, Cpl. Arbruster, and Cpl. Driesel; second row—Pfc. Garner, Sgt. Jack Cole, Cpl. Elmer Harelson, Capt. Harry L. Gans, Cpl. Cohen, Sgt. Leance, M. Sgt. John H. Conley, and Cpl. Barrett; third row—Pfc. Carr, Sgt. Brown, Cpl. Hosick, Pfc. Puckett, and Pfc. Baumunk; back row (alone)— Cpl. Audrey Hysell (picture taken outside the monastery in Heerlen, Holland, 25 February 1945, where the group was billeted) the executive officer, Lieutenant Colonel Dupre, and the personnel sergeant, Staff Sergeant Blankenship, went to Fort Benning, Georgia, to prepare for the reception of the rest of the headquarters,[180] the rest of the headquarters went on thirty days' leave before reporting to Fort Benning for preparation for shipment to the Pacific.[181] But while they were on leave, the situation in the Pacific changed much faster than expected. After the dropping of atomic bombs on Hiroshima and Nagasaki and the entry of Russia into the war, Japan surrendered. The headquarters finally reassembled on 16 August and continued their preparations for redeployment.[182] Finally, on 1 September 1945, the movement-alert notification for the 1st Medical Group was canceled.[183] The war was indeed over at last.

But things were not quite over for the group yet. As members of the headquarters were discharged or transferred to other organizations, the headquarters shrank rapidly in size. On 16 October 1945, Captain Harry L. Gans assumed command of the group from Colonel Veigel. Captain Gans had served throughout the war as the group's assistant S4 and headquarters detachment commander and now commanded the remaining three officers and ten enlisted men of the headquarters.[184] On 8 November 1945, the First Army published orders announcing that the group would be inactivated on 12 November 1945.[185] The oldest active color-bearing unit in the Army Medical Department would soon be no more.

On the morning of the 12th, Captain Gans reported to his headquarters. There, he proceeded to file his last morning report and packed the group colors for shipment to the Army's flag repository in Indianapolis. Then, he transferred himself to the 488th Motor Ambulance Company, where he assumed command. There was no inactivation ceremony, for there was no one left in the unit, and in Captain Gans' words, "there was no senior headquarters interested in what happened to the Group."[186]

V. CONCLUSIONS

The eight months that the 1st Medical Group spent in combat in the European theater in 1944 and 1945 were a learning experience for the officers and men of the headquarters. Although the group had been functioning together as a team for longer than many of their subordinate units had been in existence, and although they had frequently participated in field exercises prior to deployment that allowed the staff to practice the skills necessary for them to operate in support of combat operations, they still experienced several surprises. First, they learned that medical command and control units must maintain their mobility at all times. The 1st Medical Group, supporting two different corps predominantly composed of light infantry, relocated nine times in the period between 23 February—when the Ninth Army launched its assault crossing of the Roer—and 9 April.[187] But this does not tell the entire story of their movements, as there was a two-week lull in the battle for northern Germany as the Ninth Army prepared for its assault crossing of the Rhine. Rather, they moved five times in the twelve days between 27 February and 11 March 1945—an average of one movement every two to five days.[188]

Second, they found that the bed status of a facility (the percentage of available beds filled) was not as important as the length of surgical backlog at the facility (the time between the arrival of a patient at a medical treatment facility and the time he entered the operating room for surgical treatment) when deciding where patients should be sent for treatment.[189]

Additionally, a standard method of reporting surgical backlog within the hospitals of its command was necessary to ensure an accurate portrayal of the backlog throughout the command. Because the flow of patients was best controlled at the source—the divisional medical treatment facilities—close coordination had to be established between the group and those facilities. That ensured that patients being evacuated from the divisions would be transported to the facilities where they would receive the most rapid treatment and that ebbs and flows in casualty flow could be anticipated by the group headquarters.

Third, the staff of the 1st Medical Group learned from experience that when supporting divisions in combat, the identification of specific hospitals to support specific divisions only led to "confusion, misunderstanding, and delay"[190] in the treatment of casualties. Rather, Colonel Veigel felt that he should have control over where casualties were sent in his support area. Because he controlled the evacuation assets to move patients to, from, and between hospitals and because he had the staff and assets to keep track of the ongoing battle so as to best be able to predict future areas of patient density, he could best ensure that patients were sent to facilities that were best able to treat the patient in the shortest amount of time.

The most significant conclusion is that the key to successful health-services support operations—as exemplified by the performance of the 1st Medical Group in the campaign under study—is flexibility. This element of medical support is mentioned repeatedly in the materials used in this research. It is further reflected in the after-action reports of the 31st Medical Group, also a part of the Ninth Army, and the 68th Medical Group, a part of the First Army.[191] While basic operational principles were based on those for the employment of the medical regiment, in actual practice, there were probably as many different concepts for the employment of medical groups as there were medical group commanders.* Whether we use the World War II term "flexibility" or the AirLand Battle test of "agility," the key to successful health-services support operations on the battlefield is the ability to quickly make the best use of available assets to support a rapidly changing tactical situation.[192]

---

*No field manual detailing the use of the medical group in combat was published until after the start of the Korean War.

APPENDIX

Chain of Casualty Evacuation

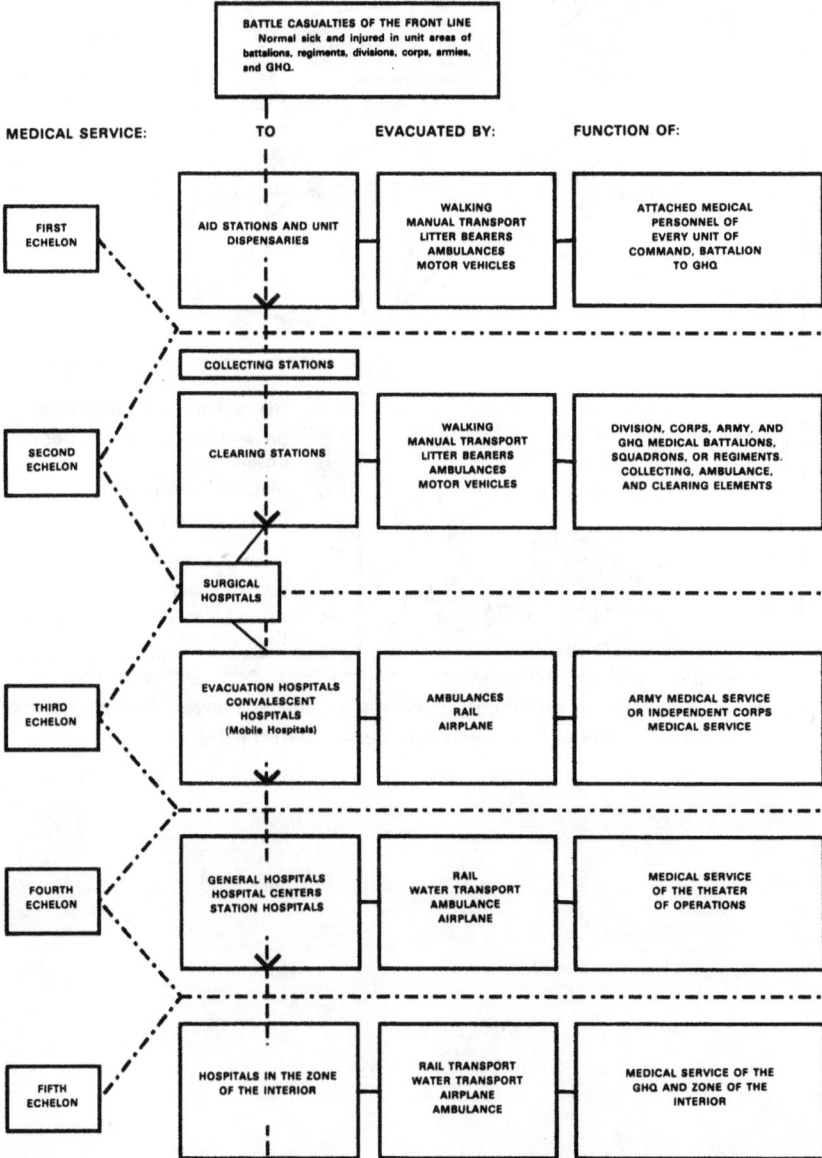

	BATTLE CASUALTIES OF THE FRONT LINE Normal sick and injured in unit areas of battalions, regiments, divisions, corps, armies, and GHQ.		
MEDICAL SERVICE:	**TO**	**EVACUATED BY:**	**FUNCTION OF:**
FIRST ECHELON	AID STATIONS AND UNIT DISPENSARIES	WALKING MANUAL TRANSPORT LITTER BEARERS AMBULANCES MOTOR VEHICLES	ATTACHED MEDICAL PERSONNEL OF EVERY UNIT OF COMMAND, BATTALION TO GHQ
	COLLECTING STATIONS		
SECOND ECHELON	CLEARING STATIONS	WALKING MANUAL TRANSPORT LITTER BEARERS AMBULANCES MOTOR VEHICLES	DIVISION, CORPS, ARMY, AND GHQ MEDICAL BATTALIONS, SQUADRONS, OR REGIMENTS. COLLECTING, AMBULANCE, AND CLEARING ELEMENTS
	SURGICAL HOSPITALS		
THIRD ECHELON	EVACUATION HOSPITALS CONVALESCENT HOSPITALS (Mobile Hospitals)	AMBULANCES RAIL AIRPLANE	ARMY MEDICAL SERVICE OR INDEPENDENT CORPS MEDICAL SERVICE
FOURTH ECHELON	GENERAL HOSPITALS HOSPITAL CENTERS STATION HOSPITALS	RAIL WATER TRANSPORT AMBULANCE AIRPLANE	MEDICAL SERVICE OF THE THEATER OF OPERATIONS
FIFTH ECHELON	HOSPITALS IN THE ZONE OF THE INTERIOR	RAIL TRANSPORT WATER TRANSPORT AIRPLANE AMBULANCE	MEDICAL SERVICE OF THE GHQ AND ZONE OF THE INTERIOR

Source: The Medical Manual *(Harrisburg, PA: The Military Service Publishing Company, 1942).*

Figure 1. Classification of field medical service by echelons (schematic)

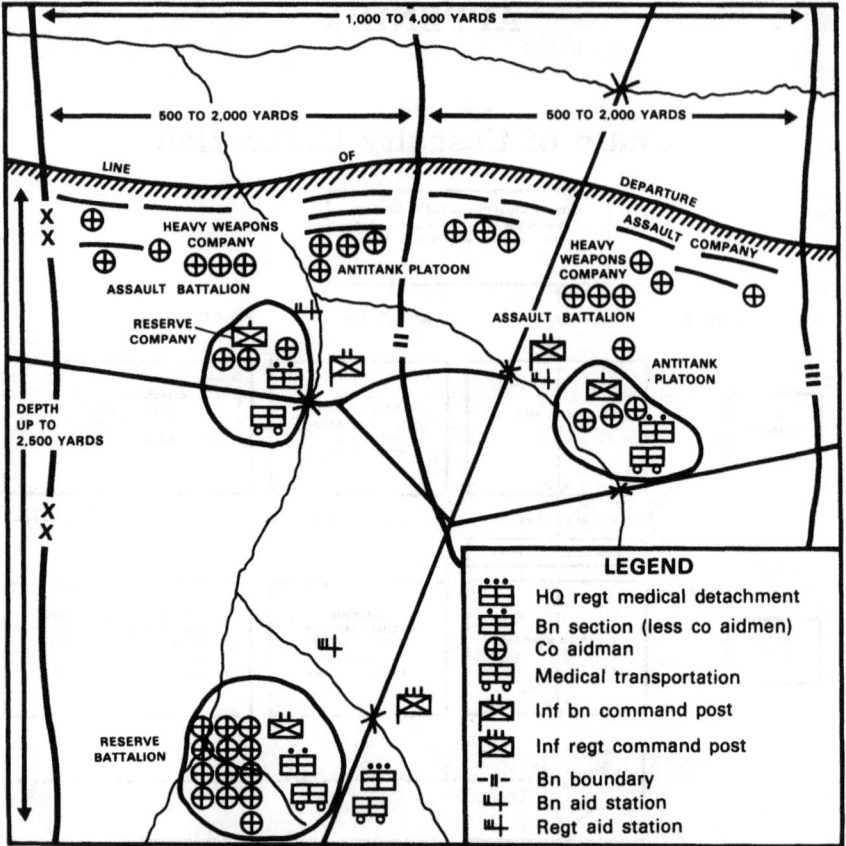

Source: The Medical Manual (Harrisburg, PA: The Military Service Publishing Company, 1942).

Figure 2. Deployment of an infantry regiment for attack, showing frontages, depth, and positions of the regimental medical detachment

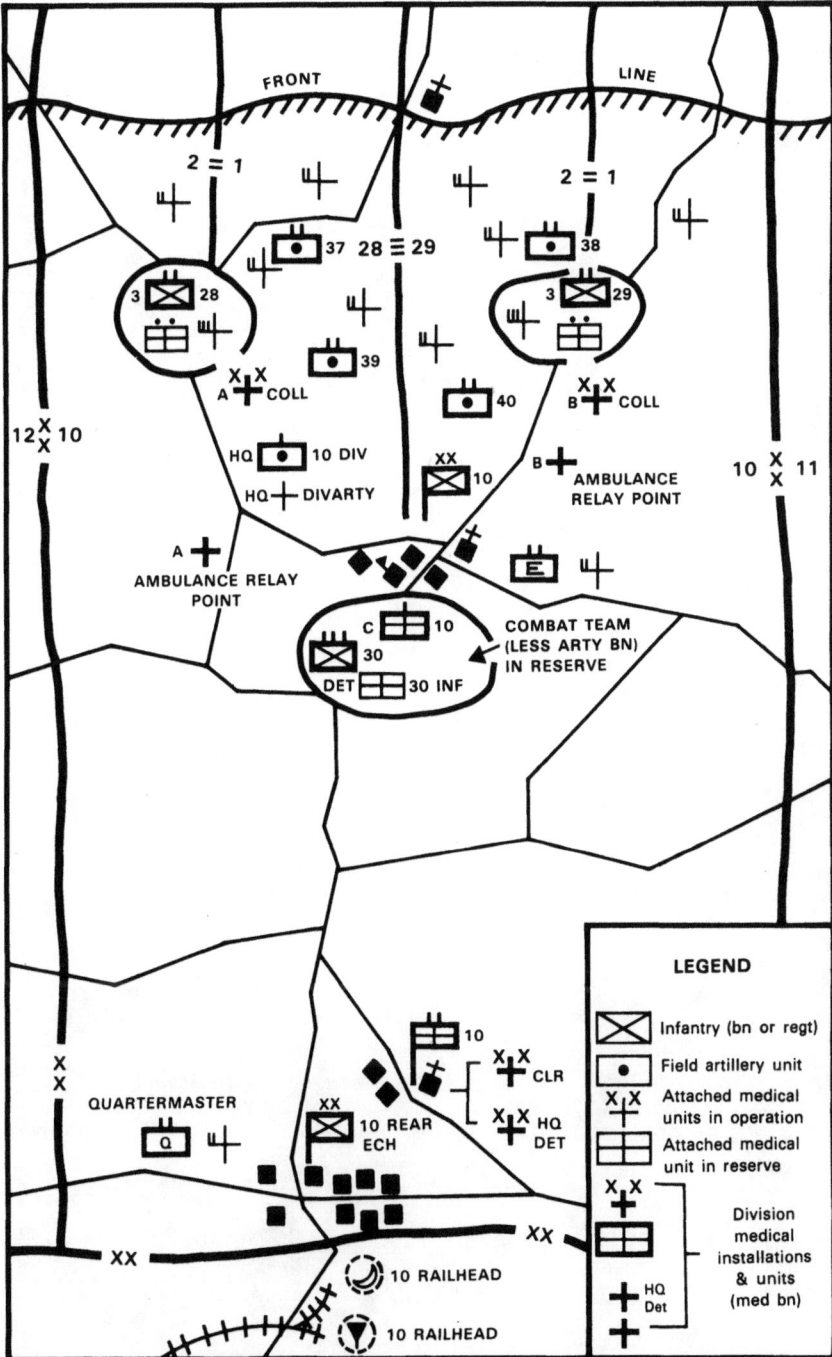

Source: The Medical Manual (Harrisburg, PA: The Military Service Publishing Company, 1942).

Figure 3. Medical support of infantry division in combat (schematic)

NOTES

1. U.S. Department of the Army, FM 90-13, *River Crossing Operations* (Washington, DC, 1986), 1-1.

2. Lorraine, Montdider-Noyon, Picardy, Aisne-Marne, St. Mihiel, and Meuse-Argonne. War Department General Order 24, 10 June 1922, 8. For a more detailed account of the activities of the 1st Sanitary Train in World War I, see Society of the First Division, *History of the First Division During the World War 1917—1919* (Philadelphia, PA: The John C. Winston Company, 1922); and Charles Lynch, Joseph H. Ford, and Frank W. Weed, *The Medical Department of the United States Army in the World War*, volume VIII, *Field Operations* (Washington, DC: U.S. Government Printing Office, 1925).

3. *History of the First Medical Regiment*, compiled February 1941 (hereafter cited as *History*), unit historical files, 1st Medical Group, Fort Hood, Texas, 12—13.

4. John B. Coates, Jr., "Thirty-One Hundred Miles with the First Medical Regiment," *Military Surgeon* 88 (1941):587—97.

5. *History*, note 3, 13.

6. Kent Roberts Greenfield, Robert R. Palmer, and Bell I. Wiley, *The Army Ground Forces—The Organization of Ground Combat Troops* (Washington, DC: Historical Division, United States Army, 1947), 351—73.

7. AG 321-Med (12 Aug 43), OB-GNGCT-M (Washington, DC: Organizational History Branch, U.S. Army Center of Military History, 14 August 1943). The separate companies resulting from the reorganization were the 407th through 412th Collecting Companies (Separate) and the 603d and 604th Clearing Companies (Separate). Additionally, the 605th Clearing Company (Separate) was activated from the assets of the 603d and 604th Clearing Companies, and the headquarters and headquarters detachments of the 163d and 164th Medical Battalions (Separate) were activated from the assets of the regimental headquarters and service company.

8. *Interview with Maj. Gen. William E. Shambora, USA (Ret), formerly Surgeon, Ninth U.S. Army, Regarding His Experiences in the European Theater of Operations—8 October 1962, Present: Maj. Gen. William E. Shambora, USA (Ret); Maj. Gen. Alvin L. Gorby; Col. John Boyd Coates, Jr., MC; Dr. Charles M. Wiltse* (hereafter cited as *Shambora Interview*), 13—18. This interview was conducted by the Army Medical Department Historical Unit as background for a yet to be published operational history of medical support in the European Theater of Operations in World War II. A copy is located in the Oral Histories Collection, U.S. Army Military History Institute, Carlisle Barracks, Pennsylvania.

9. Historical Documentation Card, William E. Shambora (Washington, DC: Special Histories Branch, U.S. Army Center of Military History).

10. Roderick M. Engbert, "A Concise Biography of Major General Paul R. Hawley." This biography was prepared by the Army Medical Department

Historical Unit in March 1966, Paul R. Hawley Papers, U.S. Army Military History Institute, Carlisle Barracks, Pennsylvania.

11. *History of the 1st Medical Group from 23 September 1944* (hereafter cited as *History from 23 Sep 44*), National Archives (NA), Records Group (RG) 407 (Records of the Office of the Adjutant General, 1917-), entry 427, box 21662, in Washington National Records Center (WNRC), 2.

12. *Annual Report—Medical Department Activities, 1st Medical Group, 1944,* 21 January 1945 (hereafter cited as *Annual Report—1944*), unit historical files, 1st Medical Group, Fort Hood, Texas, 3.

13. Harry L. Gans (Col., MSC, USA, ret.), letter to author, 16 January 1989 (hereafter cited as Gans letter), 2.

14. *History from 23 Sep 44*, 8.

15. Ibid., 16.

16. Ibid., 20.

17. Ibid., 21.

18. *Annual Report—1944*, 4.

19. Jonathan Letterman, *Medical Recollections of the Army of the Potomac* (New York: D. Appleton and Company, 1866), 162—70.

20. *Military Medical Manual*, 6th Edition, revised October 1944 (Harrisburg, PA: Military Services Publishing Company, 1945) (hereafter cited as *Military Medical Manual*), 545—46.

21. Ibid., 562.

22. Ibid., 561—62.

23. Ibid., 567—68.

24. *Journal, Surgeon's Section, Headquarters, Ninth U.S. Army*, William E. Shambora Papers, U.S. Army Military History Institute, Carlisle Barracks, Pennsylvania (hereafter cited as *Surgeon's Journal*). Numerous entries in the journal discuss the dental officer shortage in the Ninth Army and the subsequent organization of mobile dental teams as a partial solution to the problem. The originals of about one-third of the journals are located in the Special Histories Branch, U.S. Army Center of Military History, Washington, DC, and carbon copies of all journals, less enclosures, are located in the Shambora Papers at Carlisle Barracks.

25. *Military Medical Manual*, 546—47.

26. Ibid., 583—86.

27. Ibid., 601—2.

28. Ibid., 614—17.

29. *Headquarters, Ninth U.S. Army Periodic Report of Medical Department Activities, 1945 1st Semi Annual* (hereafter cited as *Surgeon's Report, 1945*), NA, RG 112 (Records of the Office of the Surgeon General [Army]), entry 54a, box 338, WNRC, section I, 3.

30. *Military Medical Manual*, 807. The separate medical clearing company was composed of 13 officers and 112 enlisted men organized into a company headquarters and 2 identical clearing platoons.

31. Ibid., 806. The separate medical collecting company was composed of 5 officers and 105 enlisted men organized into a company headquarters, a litter-bearer platoon, an ambulance platoon with 10 ambulances, and a collecting-station platoon.

32. Ibid., 822. The separate motor ambulance company was composed of four officers (all from the Medical Administrative Corps) and eighty-nine enlisted men, organized into a company headquarters and three ambulance platoons, each with ten ambulances, providing a total of thirty ambulances for the company.

33. Ibid., 804.

34. Ibid., 805.

35. Ibid., 633. The 750-bed evacuation hospital—with 47 commissioned officers, 52 nurses, a dietitian, a warrant officer, and 308 enlisted men—was designed to fulfill several missions, among them to

> Provide, as near to the front as practicable, facilities for major medical and surgical procedures in the care and treatment of all casualties.

> Provide facilities for the concentration of evacuees in such numbers and at such locations that mass evacuation by common carrier can be undertaken economically.

> Provide opportunity and facilities for the beginning of definitive treatment as early as practicable.

> Continue the sorting of casualties, under conditions more favorable for observation, and to remove from the chain of evacuation such as are, or soon will be, fit for duty.

> Prepare evacuees for extended evacuation to general hospitals at some distance to the rear.

Nurses held "equivalent ranks" to officers until June 1944 when they were commissioned. Tables of organization listed them separately from officers and were not corrected to reflect their commissioned status until after the end of the war. The wartime usage is used throughout this paper.

36. Ibid., 844.

37. Ibid., 632—33.

38. Ibid., 617—18.

39. Ibid., 644—45. The field hospital was staffed with 22 commissioned officers, 18 nurses, and 227 enlisted men organized into a headquarters with 4 commissioned officers, 3 nurses, and 19 enlisted men; it also included 3 identical hospital units, each with 6 commissioned officers, 5 nurses, and 67 enlisted men.

40. *Shambora Interview*, 51—55. To put the staffing of the field hospital's hospital unit in perspective, the table of organization for the currently

fielded mobile army surgical hospital provides 41 nurses and 16 Medical Corps officers to staff 60 beds—against the 5 Medical Corps officers and 5 nurses used to staff the 100 beds of the hospital unit of the World War II field hospital.

41. *Military Medical Manual*, 641—45.

42. Ibid., 637—41.

43. Ibid., 547.

44. Clarence McKittrick Smith, *The Medical Department: Hospitalization and Evacuation, Zone of the Interior* (Washington, DC: Office of the Chief of Military History, Department of the Army, 1956), 304—13.

45. *Military Medical Manual*, 547.

46. U.S. War Department, FM 8-10, *Medical Service of Field Units* (Washington, DC, 28 March 1942) (hereafter cited as FM 8-10), 2. While this manual predates the reorganization that replaced medical regiments with groups (and hence does not discuss their employment), it was not superseded by a revised edition until 1951.

47. Spurgeon Neel, *Medical Support of the U.S. Army in Vietnam, 1965—1970* (Washington, DC: Department of the Army, 1973), 331.

48. *Surgeon's Journal*, which notes dates and general contents of the meetings.

49. *After Action Report, XIII Corps Surgeon, February 1945*, NA, RG 407, entry 427, WNRC. This is a journal similar to the one above, which again lists attendees and contents of meetings. Colonel Schamber had served in the 1st Medical Regiment in 1938 and 1939.

50. XVI Corps Surgeon After Action Report 0001 1 March 1945 to 2400 31 March 1945, NA, RG 407, entry 427, WNRC. This is another staff journal describing the same type of meetings as the ones above.

51. *Conquer: The Story of Ninth Army 1943—1945* (Washington, DC: Infantry Journal Press, 1947) (hereafter cited as *Conquer*), 117—19.

52. Charles B. MacDonald, *The Last Offensive* (Washington, DC: U.S. Army Center of Military History, 1973) (hereafter cited as *Offensive*), 70.

53. *Conquer*, 161—63.

54. *Offensive*, 81—83.

55. Thomas R. Stone, "1630 Comes Early on the Roer," *Military Review* 53 (October 1973):3—21. A somewhat different version of this article appears as chapter 4 of Dr. Stone's Ph.D. dissertation.

56. *Conquer*, 162.

57. *Shambora Interview*, 24—32. Colonel Shambora relates that in December 1944, the Ninth Army chief of staff asked him to move one of Shambora's hospitals out of a casern in Bastogne to make room for a corps head-quarters. He told the chief of staff that he felt that a hospital should have priority due to its special requirements, and the chief agreed. Shortly afterward, he was asked to report to General Simpson, who asked him if he would move the hospital. Shambora said "no," so Simpson asked him

to see if he could find another suitable location. Shambora looked and was able to find an acceptable, if inferior, site to the one the hospital was already in—both in physical facilities and proximity to the front. (Shambora, incidentally, had his jeep stolen in the process.) Shambora did not like the site as well, but if Simpson told him to move, he would move. Then, Shambora said:

> At this time I think that the important thing that general Simpson told me, which subsequently stuck throughout the rest of the European war was that, "Bill," he said, "from now on you have first choice on any building within the whole Army area and nobody else has first choice—no matter who or what kind of building it is. Your hospitals will get first choice." "Well," I said, "that's fine."

In the end, all worked out for the best, for two days after the hospital moved, on 16 December, the Germans bombed the casern heavily, and the hospital, which was transferred to the First Army at the start of the Battle of the Bulge, ended up being ideally sited to support the First Army during the attack and subsequent counteroffensive without having to displace.

58. William H. Simpson, "Rehearsal for the Rhine," *Military Review* 25 (October 1945):20—28 (hereafter cited as "Rehearsal").

59. *After Action Report, 1st Medical Group, From 1200A 25 November to 2400A 30 November 1944* (hereafter cited as *AAR, Nov 1944*), unit historical files, 1st Medical Group, Fort Hood, Texas, 1.

60. "Death Notice of Lester P. Veigel," *Journal of the American Medical Association* 170 (29 August 1959):2, 219.

61. Louis Veigel, telephone interview with author, 31 July 1989. Louis Veigel is the late Colonel Veigel's brother.

62. General Order 12, 1st Medical Regiment, 7 August 1943, NA, RG 407, entry 427, box 21763, WNRC. After the war, Colonel Veigel transferred to the U.S. Air Force. He died of a heart attack in 1959 while serving as Surgeon of the Western Defense Command; he was fifty-four at the time of his death.

63. Biographical Sketches, 1st Medical Group, NA, RG 407, entry 427, box 21662, WNRC. This file consists of short, one-paragraph biographical sketches of the officers (except, unfortunately, Colonel Veigel) assigned to the headquarters of the 1st Medical Group Army Medical Group at the end of 1944.

64. Ibid. In the author's experience, this appears to be a prerequisite for assignment as the S3 of the 1st Medical Group. After the war, Major Prideaux returned to Portland and the banking business, eventually becoming a vice chairman of U.S. Bancorp.

65. *History from 23 Sep 44*, 11—12.

66. Biographical Data Card, John D. Dupre, Special Histories Branch, U.S. Center of Military History, Washington, DC.

67. *Report of Medical Operations, 1st Medical Group*, 1 January 1944, NA, RG 112, entry 54a, box 42, WNRC, 2—3.

68. *After Action Report, 1st Medical Group, From 0001A 1 January 1945 to 2400A 31 January 1945*, 5 February 1945 (hereafter cited as *AAR, Jan 1945*), Special Histories Branch, U.S. Army Center of Military History, Washington, DC, 2.

69. *After Action Report, 1st Medical Group, From 0001A 1 December 1944 to 2400A 31 December 1944*, 5 January 1945 (hereafter cited as *AAR, Dec 1944*), unit historical files, 1st Medical Group, Fort Hood, Texas, 2.

70. *AAR, Nov 1944*, 2.

71. *AAR, Jan 1945*, 1.

72. *Annual Report—1944*, 4.

73. "Informal Diary," in *War Diary, 1st Medical Regiment/1st Medical Group, 10 March 1942—June 1945*, NA, RG 407, entry 427, box 21762, WNRC (hereafter cited as *War Diary*). This is a two-page narrative of "a few points of interest" in January 1945. The diary itself was a book required whenever a unit was engaged in combat or field training, and it and its two companion volumes in the National Archives give a moderately detailed account of the activities of the 1st Medical Regiment and 1st Medical Group from 1922 to 1945. A microfilm copy of the diaries is in the author's possession.

74. *Annual Report—1944*, 12.

75. "Informal Diary," in *War Diary*. Unfortunately, the mattresses were infested with mice, which caused quite a nuisance for three weeks, until one member of the detachment managed to obtain some mousetraps while picking up the unit's beer ration.

76. *Annual Report—1944*, 11—12.

77. *War Diary*. Several instances of bombardment are noted in the diary.

78. *Report of Activities, 1st Medical Group, 1945—1st Semi-annual*, 5 June 1945 (hereafter cited as *Report of Activities, 1945*), Special Histories Branch, U.S. Army Center of Military History, Washington, DC, 3. While all medical units were required to make annual reports to the Office of the Surgeon General, the Surgeon of the European Theater of Operations, Major General Paul R. Hawley (himself a former commander of the 1st Medical Regiment) directed that all medical units in the European theater would prepare semiannual reports using the same format as they had used on the annual reports before they redeployed to the United States or the Pacific theater. Since many units failed to prepare annual historical reports when they were inactivated following the surrender of Japan, this move ensured that much historical information was saved that might otherwise have been lost.

79. *After Action Report, 1st Medical Group, From 0001A 1 February 1945 to 2400A 28 February 1945*, 9 March 1945 (hereafter cited as *AAR, Feb 1945*), Special Histories Branch, U.S. Army Center of Military History, Washington, DC, 1. Interestingly, the U.S. Third Army required similar reports from units prior to their deployment for southwest Asia following Operation Desert Storm.

80. *Surgeon's Report, 1945*, part III, 9.

81. Ibid. Still later, a fourth medical group, the 64th, was added to the army near the end of the war.

82. *Shambora Interview*, 47—48.

83. *Conquer*, 147—51.

84. U.S. War Department, FM 8-55, *Reference Data* (Washington, DC, 5 March 1941), 21.

85. Comments on operation of the headquarters are based on entries found in the *Unit Journal, HQ 1st Medical Group*, 12 November 1944—31 May 1945 (hereafter cited as *Unit Journal*, with appropriate date of entry), NA, RG 407, entry 427, box 21660—21661, WNRC.

86. Colonel William E. Shambora, letter to Brigadier General Frederick A. Blesse, 14 April 1943. In the William E. Shambora Papers, U.S. Army Military History Institute, Carlisle Barracks, Pennsylvania. General Blesse had been Colonel Shambora's immediate predecessor as the Army Ground Forces Surgeon (as well as a former S3 of the 1st Medical Regiment); the letter gave him informal information on what had changed in the headquarters since his departure.

87. *Shambora Interview*, 37—41. Some of the other army surgeons held the same view; others (most notably Brigadier General Joseph I. Martin of the U.S. Fifth Army in Italy) did not.

88. *Conquer*, 106.

89. *Unit Journal*, assorted entries for 12 November 1944 to 31 May 1945.

90. Ibid., entries for 25 November 1944 through 31 May 1945.

91. Ibid., assorted entries for 1 February through 1 April 1945.

92. *AAR, Feb 1945*, 3.

93. Ibid., 3.

94. Ibid.

95. Ibid., 1. The 183d Medical Battalion was composed of the 442d and 462d Medical Collecting Companies and the 626th Medical Clearing Company, while the 430th was composed of the 415th Medical Collecting Company and the 488th and 489th Motor Ambulance Companies. The 188th Medical Battalion was composed of the 463d Medical Collecting Company and the 472d Motor Ambulance Company. For an account of the Roer River crossing at the infantry-company level, see Harold P. Leinbaugh and John D. Campbell, *The Men of Company K* (New York: William Morrow and Company, 1985).

96. *Conquer*, 169.

97. *Offensive*, 183—84.

98. "Rehearsal."

99. *Conquer*, 187—89.

100. *Offensive*, 172.

101. Ibid., 173—78.

102. *Unit Journal*, entries 1—23 February 1945.

103. *AAR, Feb 1945*, 2.

104. Ibid.

105. Ibid.

106. *Period Report of Medical Department Activities, 430th Medical Battalion*, 8 June 1945 (hereafter cited as *430th Med Bn Report*), NA, RG 112, entry 54a, box 358, WNRC.

107. *Unit Journal*, entry for 23 February 1945.

108. Ibid., entry for 24 February 1945.

109. *AAR, Feb 1945*, 3.

110. *430th Med Bn Report*, 4.

111. *Report of Activities, 1945*, 2.

112. *War Diary*, entries for 27 February to 4 March 1945.

113. *430th Med Bn Report*, 4.

114. *Report of Activities from 1 January 1945 to Date, 188th Medical Battalion*, 7 June 1945 (hereafter cited as *188th Med Bn Report*), NA, RG 112, entry 54a, box 357, WNRC, 3—4.

115. *Medical Department Activities Report, 1945—1st Semi-Annual, 183rd Medical Battalion* (hereafter cited as *183d Med Bn Report*), NA, RG 112, entry 54a, box 357, WNRC, 3.

116. *After Action Report, 1st Medical Group, From 0001A 1 March 1945 to 2400A 31 March 1945*, 14 April 1945 (hereafter cited as *AAR, Mar 1945*), Special Histories Branch, U.S. Army Center of Military History, Washington, DC, 2—3

117. Ibid., 3.

118. *After Action Report, 183rd Medical Battalion, February 1945*, 5 March 1945, NA, RG 112, entry 54a, box 357, WNRC, 1.

119. *AAR, Mar 1945*, 1.

120. *Daily Record of Activities of Medical Section, Headquarters XIII Corps for Month of March 1945*, entry for 8 March 1945, NA, RG 407, entry 427, WNRC.

121. *Report of Activities, 1945*, 2.

122. *AAR, Mar 1945*, 2.

123. *430th Med Bn Report*, 2.

124. *History from 23 Sep 1944*, 5—10.

125. Malcolm D. Blankenship, letter to author, 4 April 1989. Mr. Blankenship worked in the S1 section of the group headquarters and ran the group message center, 5.

126. *Offensive*, 294—95.

127. Ibid., 295—96.

128. *Conquer*, 226—30.

129. Ibid., 230—33.

130. Ibid., 219. For more on the deception plan, see also Richard W. Stewart, "Crossing the Rhine and Irrawaddy," *Military Review* 59 (August 1989): 74—83.

131. *Unit Journal*, entry for 21 March 1945.

132. Ibid., entry for 24 March 1945.

133. *AAR, Mar 1945*, 1. The 188th Medical Battalion was composed of the 463d Medical Collecting Company and the 472d and 565th Motor Ambulance Companies, while the 430th Medical Battalion was composed of the 462d Medical Collecting Company and the 488th and 489th Motor Ambulance Companies. Removed from the group as part of the 183d Medical Battalion were the 415th and 442d Medical Collecting Companies and the 626th Medical Clearing Company.

134. *After Action Report*, 183rd Medical Battalion, March 1945, NA, RG 112, entry 54a, box 357, WNRC, 1.

135. *We Cross the Rhine—Germany, 24th March 1945*, Office of the XVI Corps Surgeon (hereafter cited as *We Cross the Rhine*), 9. A copy of this report is located in the Unit Histories Collection of the library of the U.S. Army Military History Institute, Carlisle Barracks, Pennsylvania.

136. Ibid., 10—11.

137. *Report After Action, Ninth US Army for the Period 16—31 March 1945* (hereafter cited as *Ninth Army Report*), 2. A copy of this report is located in the Unit Histories Collection of the library of the U.S. Army Military History Institute, Carlisle Barracks, Pennsylvania.

138. *Offensive*, 208—35.

139. *Ninth Army Report*, 2—3.

140. Ibid., 3.

141. Ibid., 3—4.

142. *AAR, Mar 1945*, 2.

143. *We Cross the Rhine*, 29.

144. *After Action Report, 1st Medical Group, From 0001A 1 April 1945 to 2400A 30 April 1945*, 5 May 1945 (hereafter cited as *AAR, Apr 1945*), files of the Special Histories Branch, U.S. Army Center of Military History, Washington, DC, 1.

145. *We Cross the Rhine*, 29—30.

146. *430th Med Bn Report*, 5.

147. *183d Med Bn Report*, 4.

148. *Unit Journal*, entries for 23 to 31 March 1945.

149. *430th Med Bn Report*, 5.

150. *Report of Activities, 1945*, 2.

151. *Conquer*, 269—305.

152. *AAR, Apr 1945*, 2.

153. *430th Med Bn Report*, 5.

154. Ibid., 2—3.

155. Book Message No. 117—O & T, *Procedure for Control of Uncovered German Military Hospitals*, 1 April 1945, copy included in *Surgeon's Journal*, entry for 1 April 1945, 1.

156. *AAR, Apr 1945*, 2.

157. Ibid., 2.

158. Ibid., 5.

159. Ibid., 3.

160. Ibid.

161. Ibid. The 183d Medical Battalion was composed of the 442d and 463d Medical Collecting Companies and the 626th Medical Clearing Company, while the 185th was composed of the 627th Medical Clearing Company and the ambulance platoon of the 445th Medical Collecting Company. The 430th Medical Battalion was composed of the 415th, 462d, and 481st Medical Collecting Companies; the 488th Motor Ambulance Company; and the 666th Medical Clearing Company.

162. Ibid., 3—4.

163. Ibid., 4.

164. *430th Med Bn Report*, 6—7.

165. *After Action Report, 1st Medical Group, From 0001A 1 May 1945 to 2400A 31 May 1945*, 3 June 1945 (hereafter cited as *AAR, May 1945*), files of Special Histories Branch, U.S. Army Center of Military History, Washington, DC, 2.

166. *430th Med Bn Report*, 7.

167. *AAR, May 1945*, 2.

168. Ibid., 3.

169. *Shambora Interview*, 66—69.

170. *Surgeon's Report, 1945*, section I, 3.

171. *War Diary*, entry for 24 May 1945.

172. Ibid., entry for 28 May 1945.

173. *AAR, May 1945*, 2.

174. *War Diary*, entry for 7 June 1945.

175. Ibid., entry for 11 June 1945.

176. Ibid., entry for 17 June 1945.

177. Ibid., entry for 18 June 1945.

178. Ibid.

179. Ibid., entry for 1 July 1945.

180. Malcolm D. Blankenship, letter to author, 4 April 1989.

181. *War Diary*, entry for 2 July 1945.

182. Ibid., entry for 16 August 1945.

183. Ibid., entry for 1 September 1945.

184. Gans letter, 1.

185. General Order 29, Special Troops, U.S. First Army, 8 November 1945. There is no indication of when the group transferred from the control of the U.S. Second Army to the control of the First Army, although it most likely occurred in conjunction with the move to Fort Benning.

186. Gans letter, 2.

187. *Report of Activities, 1945*, 2—3.

188. *War Diary*. See the daily entries during the time periods specified, which listed not only the movements of the group headquarters but the movements of many of the units subordinate to the group as well.

189. *AAR, Feb 1945*, 3.

190. Ibid., 3.

191. *War Diary*. Entries in the *War Diary* include regimental and group operations orders, administrative-logistics orders, and other documents and descriptive notes of the exercises in which the regiment and group participated prior to its deployment to Europe. *Annual Report of Medical Department Activities, Headquarters and Headquarters Detachment, 31st Medical Group, Period 1 January 1945 to 31 May 1945*, 26 June 1945, files of Special Histories Branch, U.S. Army Center of Military History, Washington, DC, 1—9; Francis P. Kintz and John Edgar, "Medical Groups (T/O 8-22) of First U.S. Army in the European Campaign," *Military Surgeon* 106 (1950): 34—40, 139—47, 187—92. Colonel Kintz served as commander and Major Edgar as adjutant of the 68th Medical Group throughout the European campaign.

192. FM 8-10, 28 March 1942, 16; and FM 8-55, *Planning for Health Service Support* (Washington, DC: Department of the Army, February 1985), 1—2, 1—4.

GLOSSARY

Ambulance control point. The ambulance control point consisted of a soldier stationed at a crossroads or road junction where ambulances might take one of two or more directions to reach their destination. The soldier, in communications with his higher headquarters, directed ambulances to their proper destination.

Battalion aid station. The battalion aid station provided first-echelon medical care to soldiers of its supported battalion. It was normally located in the battalion combat trains. The battalion aid station had no patient-holding capability, and patients who could not be treated and returned to duty were evacuated by one of the divisional collecting companies to the collecting station in support of the battalion's regiment.

Bed. In Army Medical Department usage, a facility is equipped with "beds" if it has Army Nurse Corps officers assigned to staff its holding facilities and "cots" if it does not. Thus, a clearing company had its holding capability expressed in number of cots, while a hospital had it expressed in beds, even though the patients in both facilities might be resting on the same type of furniture.

Division clearing station. The division clearing station was established by the clearing company of the division's medical battalion. At the clearing station, patients were triaged or sorted, and those who required care beyond the capabilities of the clearing station were prepared for transport to third-echelon treatment facilities, while those who could be returned to duty within a relatively short time, normally a few hours, would be held until released.

Division collecting station. The division collecting stations were established by the collecting companies of the division, normally with one in support of each of the division's regiments. Patients were brought to the collecting station by the soldiers of the company's litter-bearer platoon. At the station, patients were examined by a Medical Corps officer, given emergency treatment if required, and then placed on ambulances of the company's ambulance platoon for transport to the division clearing station.

Evacuation hospital. A 750-bed facility of the field army, the evacuation hospital had the mission of providing major medical facilities for the care of all types of casualties and for preparing them for return to duty or for evacuation farther to the rear. The evacuation hospital had no mobility using organic transportation assets and was essentially a fixed facility.

Evacuation hospital (semimobile). A 400-bed facility with the same mission and general capabilities of the 750-bed evacuation hospital, the evacuation hospital (semimobile) was about 25 percent mobile using organic transportation. With a trained staff, the hospital could be prepared to move within ten hours after its last patient had left and could be operational within six hours after arriving at a new location.

Field hospital. The field hospital was a medical unit designed to establish a single 400-bed hospital or three 100-bed hospitals known as hospital units. Its mission was to provide definitive surgical and medical treatment to troops in the theater of operations where fixed facilities did not exist and where the construction of fixed facilities was undesirable.

General hospital. The general hospital was a 1,000-bed medical facility found in the area under the control of the Services of Supply. It was designed and staffed to provide for the return of the maximum number of soldiers to duty within the evacuation policy established for the theater.

Medical battalion (divisional). The divisional medical battalion was responsible for providing all second-echelon health-services support to elements of the infantry division. It was organized with a headquarters, one clearing company, and three collecting companies.

Medical battalion (separate). The separate medical battalion headquarters provided command and control to form three to six subordinate medical companies. It also provided maintenance and personnel-services support to its attached units by consolidating company clerks and mechanics from its subordinate companies at battalion level.

Medical depot company. This unit, assigned to the field army, had the mission of providing medical supply, medical-equipment maintenance, and dental-appliance fabrication and repair in support of a force of up to 125,000 soldiers.

Motor ambulance company. The motor ambulance company had the mission of providing patient evacuation. To perform this mission, it was equipped with thirty ambulances, organized into three platoons of ten each. The designation "motor" was used to differentiate the company from animal-drawn ambulance companies, which were still in use by the Army at the start of World War II.

Regimental aid station. Organized much the same as a battalion aid station, the regimental aid station provided first-echelon medical care to troops located in the regimental rear area. Using its two assigned Dental Corps officers, it also provided dental care to all soldiers of the regiment. As it provided the same level of care as the battalion aid stations in its regiment, it did not normally receive patients from the regiment's battalion aid stations.

Surgeon. The term "surgeon" has two meanings in Army Medical Department usage. In general usage, and on authorization documents of medical units, the term surgeon refers to a physician who has had postgraduate training in operative procedures. In nonmedical units, the term surgeon refers to the senior Medical Corps officer in the organization, who serves as a special staff officer to the commander on matters concerning health-service support. Thus, the senior officer in a hospital is the commander, but in an infantry regiment, he is the regimental surgeon.

Surgical backlog. The time, generally measured in hours, from when a patient arrives at a medical treatment facility until he enters the operating room for surgery. Large surgical backlogs can result in increased loss of patients' lives or reduced probability of their early return to duty.

☆U.S. GOVERNMENT PRINTING OFFICE: 1992-654-001/42054